GREAT TASTES
SOUPS

First published in 2009 by Bay Books, an imprint of Murdoch Books Pty Limited
This edition published in 2010.

Murdoch Books Australia
Pier 8/9
23 Hickson Road
Millers Point NSW 2000
Phone: +61 (0) 2 8220 2000
Fax: +61 (0) 2 8220 2558
www.murdochbooks.com.au

Murdoch Books UK Limited
Erico House, 6th Floor
93–99 Upper Richmond Road
Putney, London SW15 2TG
Phone: +44 (0) 20 8785 5995
Fax: +44 (0) 20 8785 5985
www.murdochbooks.co.uk

Chief Executive: Juliet Rogers
Publishing Director: Kay Scarlett
Publisher: Lynn Lewis
Senior Designer: Heather Menzies
Designer: Wendy Inkster
Production: Kita George

ISBN: 9780681657809

PRINTED IN CHINA

IMPORTANT: Those who might be at risk from the effects of salmonella poisoning (the elderly, pregnant women, young children and those suffering from immune deficiency diseases) should consult their doctor with any concerns about eating raw eggs.

OVEN GUIDE: You may find cooking times vary depending on the oven you are using. For fan-forced ovens, as a general rule, set the oven temperature to 20°C (35°F) lower than indicated in the recipe.

GREAT TASTES

SOUPS

More than 120 easy recipes for every day

bay books

CONTENTS

SOUP BASICS

There's nothing quite like homemade soup. It's enjoyable and surprisingly easy to make if you follow a few commonsense rules, and can be dressed up or down to suit just about any occasion.

Stock secrets

While soup is ideal for using up odds and ends from the refrigerator, it is only as good as its ingredients, and the backbone of any good soup is its stock. There are several alternatives when choosing stock. You can use home-made, fresh or frozen stock available from some delicatessens or poultry shops, or tetra packs or cubes from the supermarket. The best stock will be home-made or fresh and, as it can be frozen, it is a good idea to cook up large quantities every time. Tetra packs are convenient, as are stock cubes; however, check the labels and choose cubes made from natural ingredients with no added MSG. Commercial stocks always tend to be much saltier than home-made, so taste the soup before seasoning with salt and pepper. Always season soup at the end of the cooking time, as long cooking concentrates the flavours.

Try to use the flavour stock called for in the recipe. A beef stock would be overpowering in a recipe that calls for chicken stock, although vegetarians might prefer to use vegetable stock in all their soups.

Purée and strain

Many soups are puréed before serving and there is a sensible way to go about this. Let the soup cool a little first, so that it is safe if it splashes. Cool it quickly by pouring it into a bowl, then wash the pan to take the puréed soup for reheating. Purée in either a food processor or a blender — a blender will give a finer result, though it tends to aerate the soup slightly. Always purée in batches, never filling the processor above halfway.

Occasionally, recipes ask for the soup to be strained, particularly if making the stock is part of the recipe. A fine sieve (not a colander) is usually adequate. Some clear soups need more than one straining through a sieve lined with damp muslin. If you don't have muslin, use a clean damp kitchen cloth.

Ahead of time

Many soups can be made in advance and do, in fact, benefit from overnight refrigeration as the flavours develop. Use commonsense to determine if any of the ingredients will not store well, for example if the soup has cream, add it when you are reheating for serving. The same goes for pasta; for instance, if you add the pasta to minestrone, then leave it to sit around, it will be unpleasantly soggy. Generally, soups can be kept for up to 3 days in the refrigerator, or frozen in airtight containers or freezer bags for up to 1–3 months. A lot of soups become very thick on standing and need to be diluted when reheated. Use more of the same stock, water or cream, as appropriate. The seasoning will also need to be adjusted.

Most recipes call for a heavy-based pan for making soup. This is so that the pan distributes heat evenly and prevents anything 'catching' on the bottom. A wide, shallow pan will allow too much evaporation. The recipe will state if the pan should be covered. If it is not to be covered the soup will simmer and, as the liquid evaporates off it, it will reduce down and thicken. So, if your soup is still a little thin, simply simmer it uncovered for a while. Most soups are cooked at a gentle simmer, meaning that the surface of the soup is barely moving, while a simmer means the soup will be moving faster but without bubbles breaking the surface. Boiling is when bubbles actively break the surface of the soup. Watch the soup and adjust the heat accordingly. If the recipe says to partially cover the pan, tilt the lid at an angle so that there is a gap for steam to escape.

Soup is a dish whose sum is definitely greater than its parts. And one of its most important parts is stock. A good stock makes the difference between an ordinary and a spectacular soup, giving full-bodied flavours and a sound base for the other ingredients. If you are looking at these recipes and thinking the cooking times seeming very long and it all looks like too much trouble, think again. It doesn't take long to chop up the ingredients and then you can leave your stock to simmer lazily while you get on with other things.

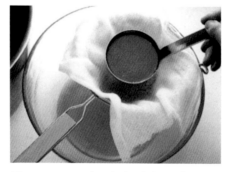

Tilt the lid at an angle if the recipe calls for a partially covered pan.

Clear soups can be strained through a sieve lined with damp muslin.

Some soups thicken on standing and need to be diluted when they are reheated.

1   **Preheat the oven** to 210°C (415°F/Gas 6–7). Put the bones in a baking dish and bake for 30 minutes, turning occasionally. Add the carrot and onion and cook for a further 20 minutes. Allow to cool.

2   **Put the bones,** carrot and onion in a large, heavy-based pan. Drain the excess fat from the baking dish and pour 250 ml (9 fl oz/ 1 cup) of water into the dish. Stir to dissolve any juices; add the liquid to the pan.

3   **Add the tomato paste,** celery and 2.5 litres (85 fl oz/ 10 cups) water. Bring to the boil, skimming the surface as required and add the bouquet garni and peppercorns. Reduce the heat to low and simmer gently for four hours. Skim the froth from the surface regularly.

4   **Ladle the stock** in batches into a fine sieve sitting over a bowl. Gently press the solids with a ladle to extract all the liquid. Discard the bones and vegetables and set aside to cool. Refrigerate until cold and spoon off any fat that has set on top. At this stage you can reduce the stock to concentrate its flavour (dilute before using) and store in the refrigerator for up to 2 days or in the freezer for up to 6 months.

BEEF STOCK

2 kg (4 lb) beef bones

2 unpeeled carrots, chopped

2 unpeeled onions, quartered

2 tablespoons tomato paste

2 sticks celery, leaves included, chopped

1 bouquet garni

12 black peppercorns

1   **Put the chicken bones,** onion, carrot, celery and 3.5 litres (118 fl oz/ 14 cups) of water in a large, heavy-based pan. Bring slowly to the boil. Skim the surface as required and add the bouquet garni and peppercorns. Reduce the heat to low and simmer gently for 3 hours. Skim the froth from the surface regularly.

2   **Ladle the stock** in batches into a fine sieve sitting over a bowl. Gently press the solids with a ladle to extract all the liquid. Let the stock cool, then refrigerate until cold and spoon off any fat that has set on the top. At this stage you can reduce the stock to concentrate its flavour (dilute before using) and store in the refrigerator for up to 2 days or in the freezer for up to 6 months.

CHICKEN STOCK

2 kg (4 lb) chicken bones

2 unpeeled onions, quartered

2 unpeeled carrots, chopped

2 sticks celery, leaves included, chopped

1 bouquet garni

12 black peppercorns

1   **Place the fish bones,** celery, onion, carrot, leek and 2 litres (70 fl oz/8 cups) water in a large, heavy-based pan. Bring slowly to the boil. Skim the surface as required and add the bouquet garni and peppercorns. Reduce the heat to low and simmer very gently for 20 minutes. Skim the froth from the surface regularly.

2   **Ladle the stock** in batches into a sieve line with damp muslin sitting over a bowl. To keep a clear fish stock, do not press the solids, but simply allow the stock to strain undisturbed. Allow to cool, then store in the refrigerator for up to 2 days or in the freezer for up to 6 months.

FISH STOCK

2 kg (4 lb) chopped fish bones, heads and tails

1 stick celery, leaves included, roughly chopped

1 onion, chopped

1 unpeeled carrot, chopped

1 leek, sliced

1 bouquet garni

12 black peppercorns

SOUP BASICS

VEGETABLE STOCK

1 tablespoon oil

1 onion, chopped

2 leeks, chopped

4 carrots, chopped

2 parsnips, chopped

4 sticks celery, leaves included, chopped

2 bay leaves

1 bouquet garni

4 unpeeled garlic cloves

8 black peppercorns

1 Heat the oil in a large, heavy-based pan and add the onion, leek, carrot, parsnip and celery. Cover and cook for 5 minutes without colouring. Add 3 litres (118 fl oz/ 12 cups) of water. Bring to the boil. Skim the surface if required, and add the bay leaves, bouquet garni, garlic and peppercorns. Reduce the heat to low and simmer for 1 hour. Skim the froth from the surface of the stock regularly.

2 Ladle the stock in batches into a fine sieve sitting over a bowl. Gently press the solids to extract all the liquid.

3 Allow the stock to cool, then refrigerate until cold and spoon off any fat that has set on the top. At this stage you can reduce the stock to concentrate its flavour (dilute before using) and store in the refrigerator for up to 2 days or in the freezer for up to 6 months.

SOUP EXTRAS

If you are preparing soup to serve as a dinner party starter or as a main course meal for the family, liven it up a little by adding bowls of accompaniments in the centre of the table. People can pick and choose what to add to their own bowl of soup. Croutons and garlic snippets are a delicious way to add extra texture and interest to just about any soup. Rouille and aioli are best known as creamy, garlicky toppings for fish soups. Harissa is great for spicing up pumpkin soup and pesto is perfect on thick vegetable soups.

Aioli

Put 2 egg yolks in a food processor. Add 3 peeled, crushed cloves of garlic and 2 teaspoons lemon juice and process for 20 seconds. With the motor running add 250 ml (9 fl oz/ 1 cup) light olive oil in a thin steady stream and continue processing until the mixture is thick and creamy. Add 2 extra teaspoons of lemon juice and season to taste. Aioli is served in dollops on top of soups and can be stored in an airtight container in the refrigerator for up to 3 weeks.

Croutons

Discard the crusts from 3–4 slices of white or brown bread. Combine 2–3 tablespoons olive oil and 1–2 peeled, crushed garlic cloves in a small bowl, then use to brush both sides of the bread. Cut the bread into small cubes and put them on an baking tray. Bake in a preheated 180°C (350°F/Gas 4) oven for 10–15 minutes, or until golden. Allow to cool before serving.

VARIATIONS: Omit the garlic or add 1 teaspoon of any ground spice to the oil for an alternative flavour. Croutons can also be made without using any oil. Simply toast the bread cubes in the oven until golden.

Garlic snippets

Trim the crusts from 3 slices of white or brown bread and cut the bread into small cubes. Heat 60 ml (2 fl oz/¼ cup) olive oil in a small, heavy-based pan. Add 1–2 crushed cloves of garlic. When the oil is moderately hot add the bread cubes in batches. Cook until golden and crisp, then remove from the pan with a slotted spoon and leave to drain on paper towels while frying the rest. Sprinkle over soup.

Harissa

Split 100 g (3½ oz) dried red chillies in half and remove the seeds—wear rubber or cotton gloves to do this or later you'll rub your eyes or mouth and find them smarting with hot chilli. Place the chillies in hot water to soften and rehydrate slightly. Drain the chillies and put them in a food processor or blender with 6 garlic cloves, 4 tablespoons salt, 50 g (1¾ oz/½ cup) of ground coriander and 35 g (1¼ oz/⅓ cup) of ground cumin. Process for 30 seconds. Add 170 ml (5¾ fl oz/⅔ cup) of olive oil in a thin steady stream, processing as you do so until the mixture forms a paste. Store in an airtight screw-top jar in the refrigerator. Add sufficient Harissa to enhance the flavour of the soup, stirring in a little at a time.

Parmesan triangle croutons

Preheat the oven to 180°C (350°F/Gas 4). Lightly grease a baking tray. Remove the crusts from 4 slices of bread and cut the slices in half diagonally. Cut each triangle in half and then in half again so that you end up with 8 small triangles. Combine 80 ml (2¾ fl oz/⅓ cup) olive oil with 50 g (1¾ oz/ ⅓ cup) finely grated parmesan. Add the triangles and toss in the mixture. When you add the parmesan to the oil most of the oil will be absorbed, but you should have enough to coat the triangles. Place the triangles on a lightly greased baking tray. Bake for 10–15 minutes, or until golden. Turn once during baking. Some triangles may be ready before others; if this is the case, remove the golden ones and continue to cook the rest.

Pesto

Put 2–3 garlic cloves, 60 g (2¼ oz/2 cups) of fresh basil leaves, 50 g (1¾ oz/½ cup) of freshly grated parmesan cheese, 2 tablespoons toasted pinenuts and 125 ml (4 fl oz/½ cup) of olive oil in a food processor. Process to form a paste, adding a little extra oil to thin if necessary. Spoon the pesto sparingly over soup in serving bowls. Store in an airtight, screw-top jar. Pack the pesto firmly into the jar and pour in enough extra olive oil to cover the surface. Refrigerate for up to 2 weeks.

Roast garlic crostini

Preheat the oven to 180°C (350°F/Gas 4). Wrap 2 garlic bulbs separately in foil. Bake for 1 hour, or until the garlic feels very soft to touch. Cool. Cut 1 long bread stick diagonally into twenty 2 cm (¾ inch) thick slices. Lay a single layer on a large baking tray and brush with 3 tablespoons olive oil. Bake for 10 minutes, or until crisp and golden. Remove any that brown too quickly. Cut the tips off the garlic and squeeze ou the flesh. Spread the garlic paste on the bread, sprinkle with a few thyme leaves, salt and freshly ground black pepper. Drizzle on a little extra olive oil, if you want.

NOTE: The garlic becomes very sweet when roasted. Roast an extra garlic bulb if you want more paste.

Rocket and sun-dried tomato pesto

Add 70 g (2¼ oz/2 cups) finely shredded rocket leaves to a food processor. Add 2 crushed cloves garlic and 50 g (1¾ oz/½ cup) finely grated Parmesan. Finely chop 35 g (1¼ oz/¼ cup) sun-dried tomatoes and add to the rocket. Process until finely chopped. Add 60 ml (2 fl oz/¼ cup) olive oil and process again until well combined. Good with most vegetable soups.

Rouille

Remove the crusts from 4 thick slices of white bread. Put the bread in a bowl and just cover with water. Leave to soak for 5 minutes then drain, squeezing out the water. Put the bread in a food processor with 4 garlic cloves, 2 chopped red chillies, 2 egg yolks, salt and pepper. Process for 20 seconds and then, with the motor still running, add 185 ml (6 fl oz/¾ cup) of olive oil in a thin steady stream. Process until thick and creamy, adding 1 small peeled red capsicum (pepper) if you like. Serve in dollops on top of fish soups.

HINT: To peel a capsicum, cut in half and remove the seeds and membrane. Brush the skin with a little oil and grill (broil), skin side up, under high heat until the skin blackens. Leave to cool under a clean tea towel, then peel away the skin and discard.

Sun-dried tomato and olive lavash bites

Preheat the oven to 190°C (375°F/Gas 5). Soften 40 g (1¼ oz) butter and place in a small bowl. Add 2 tablespoons finely chopped sun-dried tomato, 1 tablespoon finely chopped olives, 2 crushed cloves garlic and 2 tablespoons shredded basil. Mix well. Spread the mixture over 1 slice of lavash bread. Cut the lavash into strips then into small triangles. Bake for 5–10 minutes. Watch carefully as they can overbrown quickly.

Yoghurt and herb stir-in

Combine 185 g (6 oz/¾ cup) thick natural yoghurt with 2 cloves crushed garlic, 3 tablespoons finely chopped mint and 2 tablespoons finely chopped coriander. Stir through 1 tablespoon lemon juice and season well. Add a generous spoonful to Borscht, Mulligatawny or Roast pumpkin soup.

BEEF, LAMB & PORK

CAULIFLOWER, CANNELLINI AND PROSCIUTTO SOUP

SERVES 4

2 tablespoons olive oil

100 g (3½ oz/about 8 slices) prosciutto, chopped

1 onion, chopped

1 garlic clove, crushed

800 g (1 lb 12 oz) cauliflower, cut into small florets

800 g (1 lb 12 oz) tinned cannellini beans, drained

125 ml (4 fl oz/½ cup) thick cream

snipped chives, to serve

1 **Heat 1 tablespoon** of the oil in a large saucepan over medium–high heat. Add the prosciutto and fry, stirring often, until crisp. Transfer half the prosciutto to a plate lined with paper towel, leaving the rest in the saucepan.

2 **Reduce the heat** to medium. Add the remaining oil and the onion to the saucepan and fry for 5 minutes, or until softened. Add the garlic and cauliflower florets and fry for 3 minutes.

3 **Add the cannellini beans** and 1 litre (35 fl oz/4 cups) of water and season well with salt and freshly ground black pepper. Bring to the boil, then reduce the heat and simmer, covered, for 15 minutes, or until the cauliflower is tender. Set aside to cool for 10 minutes.

4 **Using an immersion blender** fitted with the chopping blade, whizz the soup for 25 seconds, or until smooth. Season with salt and plenty of freshly ground black pepper. Stir through the cream and gently reheat the soup. Serve immediately, with the reserved crisp prosciutto and the chives sprinkled on top.

VIETNAMESE PORK AND PRAWN BALL SOUP

SERVES 4

PORK AND PRAWN BALLS

2 garlic cloves, roughly chopped

1 lemongrass stem, white part only, sliced

300 g (10½ oz) pork spareribs, skin and bones removed, cut into chunks

125 g (4½ oz) raw king prawns (shrimp), peeled and deveined

1 small handful coriander (cilantro) leaves

2 teaspoons fish sauce

1.5 litres (52 fl oz/6 cups) chicken stock

1 lemongrass stem, white part only, sliced

1 small red chilli, sliced (seeded if preferred)

8 raw prawns (shrimp), peeled and deveined, leaving the tails intact

100 g (3½ oz) bean vermicelli noodles (cellophane noodles)

1–2 teaspoons fish sauce, to taste

60 ml (2 fl oz/¼ cup) lime juice

90 g (3¼ oz) bean sprouts, trimmed

1 handful Vietnamese mint, to serve

1 handful coriander (cilantro) leaves, to serve

1 **To make the pork and prawn balls,** put the garlic, lemon grass and pork in a small processor fitted with the metal blade and whizz for 20–35 seconds, or until finely chopped, occasionally scraping down the side of the processor bowl. Add the prawns, coriander and fish sauce and whizz in short bursts until the prawns are chopped but still large enough to give the balls some texture. Using moistened hands, roll 2 teaspoons of mixture at a time into small balls.

2 **Heat the stock** in a saucepan, add the lemon grass and chilli and bring to the boil. Add the pork and prawn balls and simmer for 5 minutes. Add the prawns and noodles and simmer over low heat for 1–2 minutes, or until the prawns have a tinge of orange and are almost cooked. Add the fish sauce, to taste, and lime juice.

3 **Ladle the soup** into four bowls and serve the bean sprouts, Vietnamese mint and coriander on top.

Note: Use pork spareribs with good layers of meat and fat.

PASTA, PANCETTA AND BEAN SOUP

SERVES 4

200 g (7 oz/1 cup) dried borlotti beans

3 tablespoons olive oil

90 g (3¼ oz) pancetta or bacon, finely diced

1 onion, finely chopped

2 garlic cloves, crushed

1 celery stalk, thinly sliced

1 carrot, diced

1 bay leaf

1 rosemary sprig

1 flat-leaf (Italian) parsley sprig

400 g (14 oz) tinned chopped tomatoes, drained

1.625 litres (55 fl oz/6½ cups) vegetable stock

2 tablespoons finely chopped flat-leaf (Italian) parsley

150 g (5½ oz) ditalini or other small dried pasta

extra virgin olive oil, to drizzle

freshly grated parmesan cheese, to serve

1 Put the borlotti beans in a large bowl, cover with cold water and leave to soak overnight. Drain and rinse.

2 Heat the oil in a large saucepan over medium heat. Add the pancetta, onion, garlic, celery and carrot and cook for 5 minutes, or until golden. Season with black pepper. Add the bay leaf, rosemary, parsley, tomato, stock and beans and bring to the boil. Reduce the heat and simmer for 1½ hours, or until the beans are tender. Add more boiling water if necessary to maintain the liquid level.

3 Discard the bay leaf, rosemary and parsley sprigs. Scoop out 250 ml (9 fl oz/1 cup) of the bean mixture and purée in a food processor or blender. Return to the pan, season and add the parsley and pasta. Simmer for 6 minutes, or until the pasta is al dente. Remove from the heat and set aside for 10 minutes. Serve drizzled with extra virgin olive oil and garnished with parmesan.

BORLOTTI BEAN AND ITALIAN SAUSAGE SOUP

SERVES 4

2 tablespoons olive oil

3 thin Italian sausages

100 g (3½ oz) thickly sliced pancetta, cut into 5 mm x 2 cm (¼ inch x ¾ inch) strips

2 onions, chopped

1 leek, white part only, sliced

2 garlic cloves, chopped

2 celery stalks, chopped

2 carrots, chopped

2 large thyme sprigs

1 litre (35 fl oz/4 cups) chicken stock or vegetable stock

400 g (14 oz) tinned borlotti (cranberry) beans, rinsed and drained

410 g (14½ oz) tinned diced tomatoes

2 large handfuls flat-leaf (Italian) parsley, chopped

1 Heat a little of the oil in a large frying pan over medium heat. Fry the sausages for 5–6 minutes, or until browned all over. Add the pancetta halfway through cooking. Remove from the heat and set aside.

2 Heat the remaining oil in a large heavy-based saucepan and add the onion, leek, garlic, celery and carrot. Stir for 2 minutes to coat the vegetables in the oil. Reduce the heat, cover and simmer, stirring occasionally, for 10 minutes. Do not allow the vegetables to brown.

3 Add the thyme sprigs and stock. Slowly bring to the boil, then reduce the heat and simmer, covered, for 20 minutes. Add the beans and remove the thyme sprigs. Remove the saucepan from the heat.

4 Using an immersion blender fitted with the chopping blade, whizz for 30 seconds, or until the soup is roughly puréed but still has some texture.

5 Dice the sausages and add them to the soup along with the pancetta and diced tomatoes. Gently reheat the soup. Stir through the parsley and season with plenty of salt and freshly ground black pepper.

GRILLED ITALIAN SAUSAGE AND VEGETABLE SOUP

SERVES 4

500 g (1 lb 2 oz) Italian pork sausages

200 g (7 oz) piece speck (see Note)

1 tablespoon olive oil

1 large onion, chopped

3 garlic cloves, crushed

1 celery stalk, cut in half and sliced

1 large carrot, cut into 1 cm
(½ inch) cubes

bouquet garni (1 parsley sprig, 1 oregano
sprig, 2 bay leaves)

1 small red chilli, halved lengthways

400 g (14 oz) tinned chopped tomatoes

1.75 litres (59 fl oz/7 cups) chicken stock

300 g (10½ oz) Brussels sprouts, cut in
half from top to base

300 g (10½ oz) green beans, cut into
3 cm (1¼ inch) lengths

300 g (10½ oz) shelled broad beans,
fresh or frozen

2 tablespoons chopped flat-leaf
(Italian) parsley

1 Grill (broil) the sausages under a hot grill (broiler) for 8–10 minutes, turning occasionally, or until brown. Remove and cut into 3 cm (1¼ inch) lengths. Trim and reserve the fat from the speck, then dice the speck.

2 Heat the oil in a large saucepan over medium heat. Add the speck and reserved speck fat and cook for 2–3 minutes, or until golden. Add the onion, garlic, celery and carrot, reduce the heat to low and cook for 6–8 minutes, or until softened. Discard the remains of the speck fat.

3 Stir in the sausages, bouquet garni, chilli and chopped tomato and cook for 5 minutes. Add the stock, bring to the boil, then reduce the heat and simmer for 1 hour. Add the Brussels sprouts, green beans and broad beans and simmer for 30 minutes. Discard the bouquet garni, then stir in the parsley. Season to taste. Divide among four bowls and serve.

Note: Speck is cured smoked ham or pork belly. It has a strong taste and is usually cut into small pieces and used as a flavour base.

RAVIOLI BROTH WITH LEMON AND BABY SPINACH

STOCK

1.5 kg (3 lb 5 oz) chicken bones (necks, backs, wings)

2 large leeks, chopped

2 large carrots, chopped

2 large celery stalks, chopped

6 lemon thyme sprigs

4 flat-leaf (Italian) parsley sprigs

10 black peppercorns

350 g (12 oz) fresh veal ravioli

2 strips lemon zest (6 cm/2½ inches long), white pith removed

150 g (5½ oz) baby English spinach leaves, stems removed

½ teaspoon lemon oil

1–2 tablespoons lemon juice

35 g (1¼ oz/⅓ cup) shaved parmesan cheese, to garnish

1 **Place the chicken bones** in a large pan with 3 litres (102 fl oz/12 cups) cold water. Bring to a simmer over medium–low heat (do not boil) for 30 minutes, removing any scum that rises to the surface. Add the remaining stock ingredients and simmer, partially covered, for 3 hours. Strain through a fine sieve and cool. Cover and refrigerate overnight. Remove the layer of fat on the surface.

2 **Place the stock** in a large saucepan and bring to the boil. Add the ravioli and zest and cook for 3–5 minutes, or until the ravioli floats to the top and is tender. Stir in the spinach and season. Discard the zest and, just before serving, stir in the lemon oil (to taste) and lemon juice. Garnish with the shaved parmesan.

SPAGHETTI AND MEATBALL SOUP

SERVES 4

150 g (5½ oz) spaghetti, broken into
8 cm (3 inch) lengths

1.5 litres (52 fl oz/6 cups) beef stock

3 teaspoons tomato paste (concentrated
purée)

400 g (14 oz) tinned chopped tomatoes

3 tablespoons basil leaves, torn

shaved parmesan cheese, to garnish

MEATBALLS

1 tablespoon oil

1 onion, finely chopped

2 garlic cloves, crushed

500 g (1 lb 2 oz) lean minced
(ground) beef

3 tablespoons finely chopped flat-leaf
(Italian) parsley

3 tablespoons fresh breadcrumbs

2 tablespoons finely grated
parmesan cheese

1 egg, lightly beaten

1 Cook the spaghetti in a large saucepan of boiling water according to packet instructions until al dente. Drain. Put the stock and 500 ml (17 fl oz/2 cups) water in a large saucepan and slowly bring to a simmer.

2 Meanwhile, to make the meatballs, heat the oil in a small frying pan over medium heat and cook the onion for 2–3 minutes, or until soft. Add the garlic and cook for 30 seconds. Allow to cool.

3 Combine the mince, parsley, breadcrumbs, parmesan, egg, the onion mixture, and salt and pepper. Roll a heaped teaspoon of mixture into a ball, making 40 balls in total.

4 Stir the tomato paste and tomato into the beef stock and simmer for 2–3 minutes. Drop in the meatballs, return to a simmer and cook for 10 minutes, or until cooked through. Stir in the spaghetti and basil to warm through. Season, garnish with shaved parmesan and serve.

VIETNAMESE BEEF SOUP

SERVES 4

400 g (14 oz) rump steak, trimmed
½ onion
1½ tablespoons fish sauce
1 star anise
1 cinnamon stick
pinch ground white pepper
1.5 litres (52 fl oz/6 cups) beef stock
300 g (10½ oz) fresh thin rice noodles
3 spring onions (scallions), thinly sliced
15 g (½ oz) Vietnamese mint leaves
90 g (3¼ oz) bean sprouts
1 small white onion, cut in half and thinly sliced
1 small red chilli, thinly sliced on the diagonal
lemon wedges, to serve

1 Wrap the rump steak in plastic wrap and freeze for 40 minutes.

2 Meanwhile, put the onion, fish sauce, star anise, cinnamon stick, pepper, stock and 500 ml (17 fl oz/2 cups) water in a large saucepan. Bring to the boil, then reduce the heat, cover and simmer for 20 minutes. Discard the onion, star anise and cinnamon stick.

3 Cover the noodles with boiling water and gently separate the strands. Drain and refresh under cold water.

4 Remove the meat from the freezer and thinly slice it across the grain.

5 Divide the noodles and spring onion among four deep bowls. Top with the beef, mint, bean sprouts, onion and chilli. Ladle the hot broth over the top and serve with the lemon wedge.

Note: In Vietnam, noodle soups are called pho—beef noodle soup, pho bo, is one of the most popular.

MOROCCAN LAMB, CHICKPEA AND CORIANDER SOUP

SERVES 4–6

165 g (5¾ oz/¾ cup) dried chickpeas

1 tablespoon olive oil

850 g (1 lb 14 oz) boned lamb leg, cut into 1 cm (½ inch) cubes

1 onion, chopped

2 garlic cloves, crushed

½ teaspoon ground cinnamon

½ teaspoon ground turmeric

½ teaspoon ground ginger

4 tablespoons chopped coriander (cilantro) leaves

800 g (1 lb 12 oz) tinned chopped tomatoes

1 litre (35 fl oz/4 cups) chicken stock

160 g (5¾ oz/⅔ cup) dried red lentils, rinsed

coriander (cilantro) leaves, to garnish

1 **Soak the chickpeas** in cold water overnight. Drain and rinse well.

2 **Heat the oil in a large saucepan** over high heat and brown the lamb in batches for 2–3 minutes. Reduce the heat to medium, return the lamb to the pan with the onion and garlic and cook for 5 minutes. Add the spices, season and cook for 2 minutes. Add the coriander, tomato, stock and 500 ml (17 fl oz/2 cups) water and bring to the boil over high heat.

3 **Add the lentils** and chickpeas and simmer, covered, over low heat for 1½ hours. Uncover and cook for 30 minutes, or until the lamb is tender and the soup is thick. Season. Garnish with coriander.

PORK AND BUTTERED CORN RAMEN SOUP

SERVES 4

200 g (7 oz) Chinese barbecued pork (char sui) fillet in one piece

2 small fresh corn cobs (550 g/1 lb 4 oz)

200 g (7 oz) dried ramen noodles

2 teaspoons peanut oil

1 teaspoon grated ginger

1.5 litres (52 fl oz/6 cups) chicken stock

2 tablespoons mirin

2 spring onions (scallions), sliced on the diagonal

20 g (¾ oz) unsalted butter

1 spring onion (scallion), extra, sliced on the diagonal

1 Cut the pork into thin slices and remove the corn kernels from the cob using a sharp knife.

2 Bring a large saucepan of water to the boil, add the ramen noodles and cook for 4 minutes, or until tender. Drain, then rinse in cold water.

3 Heat the oil in a large saucepan over high heat. Stir-fry the grated ginger for 1 minute. Add the chicken stock and mirin and bring to the boil. Reduce the heat and simmer for 8 minutes.

4 Add the pork slices to the liquid and cook for 5 minutes, then add the corn kernels and spring onion and cook for a further 4–5 minutes, or until the kernels are tender.

5 Separate the noodles by running them under hot water, then divide among four deep bowls. Ladle on the soup, then place 1 teaspoon butter on each serving. Garnish with the extra spring onion and serve at once.

Note: This soup is traditionally served with the butter on top. However, for a healthier option, it is also quite delicious without the butter.

OXTAIL SOUP WITH STOUT AND VEGETABLES

SERVES 4

2 kg (4 lb 8 oz) oxtails, trimmed

2 tablespoons vegetable oil

2 onions, finely chopped

1 leek, finely chopped

2 carrots, diced

1 celery stalk, diced

2 garlic cloves, crushed

2 bay leaves

2 tablespoons tomato paste
(concentrated purée)

1 thyme sprig

2 flat-leaf (Italian) parsley sprigs

3.5 litres (119 fl oz/14 cups) chicken
stock

375 ml (13 fl oz/1½ cups) stout

2 tomatoes, seeded and diced

100 g (3½ oz) cauliflower florets

100 g (3½ oz) green beans

100 g (3½ oz) broccoli florets

100 g (3½ oz) asparagus, cut into
3 cm (1¼ inch) lengths

1 **Preheat the oven** to 200°C (400°F/Gas 6). Place the oxtails in a baking dish and bake for 1 hour, turning occasionally, or until dark golden. Leave to cool.

2 **Heat the oil** in a large saucepan over medium heat and cook the onion, leek, carrot and celery for 3–4 minutes, or until soft. Stir in the garlic, bay leaves and tomato paste, then add the oxtails, thyme and parsley.

3 **Add the stock** and bring to the boil over high heat. Reduce the heat and simmer for 3 hours, or until the oxtails are tender and the meat falls off the bone. Skim off any scum that rises to the surface. Remove the oxtails and cool slightly.

4 **Take the meat off the bones** and discard any fat or sinew. Roughly chop and add to the soup with the stout, tomato and 500 ml (17 fl oz/2 cups) water. Add the vegetables and simmer for 5 minutes, or until the vegetables are tender. Season.

PEA AND HAM SOUP

SERVES 6–8

500 g (1 lb 2 oz/2¼ cups) yellow or green split peas

1½ tablespoons olive oil

2 onions, chopped

1 carrot, diced

3 celery stalks, finely chopped

1 kg (2 lb 4 oz) ham bones or a smoked ham hock, chopped (see Note)

1 bay leaf

2 thyme sprigs

lemon juice, to taste (optional)

1   Place the split peas in a large bowl, cover with cold water and soak for 6 hours. Drain well.

2   Heat the oil in a large saucepan, add the onion, carrot and celery and cook over low heat for 6–7 minutes, or until the vegetables are soft but not brown.

3   Add the peas, ham bones, bay leaf, thyme and 2.5 litres (85 fl oz/10 cups) cold water and bring to the boil. Reduce the heat and simmer, stirring occasionally, for 2 hours, or until the peas are tender, removing any scum that rises to the surface. Remove the bay leaf and thyme and discard them.

4   Remove the ham bones from the soup, cool slightly, then remove the meat from the bones and discard the bones. Return the ham to the soup and reheat. Season to taste with pepper and lemon juice, if desired.

Notes: Ask your butcher to chop the ham bones for you. For a smoother texture, the soup can be cooled and processed once the ham bones have been removed. Return the meat to the puréed soup.

CHESTNUT, PANCETTA AND CABBAGE SOUP

SERVES 4

200 g (7 oz) cavolo nero or
 savoy cabbage

2 tablespoons olive oil

1 onion, finely chopped

130 g (4½ oz) pancetta or smoked
 bacon, diced

2 garlic cloves, chopped

2 tablespoons rosemary, finely chopped

200 g (7 oz) cooked, peeled chestnuts
 roughly chopped

200 ml (7 fl oz/¾ cup) red wine

4 crostini

extra virgin olive oil and grated
 parmesan cheese, to serve

1 **Remove** any thick stems from the cavolo nero and roughly chop the leaves. Wash well and cook in 1.5 litres (52 fl oz/ 6 cups) of boiling water for about 10 minutes, or until the stems are tender. Drain in a colander over a large bowl to reserve the cooking water.

2 **Using the same saucepan,** heat the olive oil and cook the onion and pancetta over medium-high heat until the onion is soft and the pancetta lightly browned. Add the garlic and rosemary and cook for a few more minutes.

3 **Add the chestnuts** and stir to infuse the flavours, then add the cabbage and season with salt and pepper. Add the wine, bring to the boil and cook for a couple of minutes. Finally add the reserved cabbage water, bring to the boil and then simmer for 10 minutes.

4 **Purée** one-third of the soup, leaving the remainder unpuréed to give the dish a little texture. Serve the soup hot with crostini on top, drizzled with a little olive oil and sprinkled with parmesan.

WINTER LAMB SHANK SOUP

SERVES 4

1 tablespoon olive oil

1.25 kg (2 lb 12 oz) lamb shanks

2 onions, chopped

4 garlic cloves, chopped

250 ml (9 fl oz/1 cup) red wine

2 bay leaves

1 tablespoon chopped rosemary

2.5 litres (85 fl oz/10 cups) beef stock

425 g (15 oz) tinned crushed tomatoes

165 g (5¾ oz/¾ cup) pearl barley, rinsed
    and drained

1 large carrot, diced

1 potato, diced

1 turnip, diced

1 parsnip, diced

2 tablespoons redcurrant jelly (optional)

1   Heat the oil in a large saucepan over high heat. Cook the lamb shanks for 2–3 minutes, or until brown. Remove.

2   Add the onion to the pan and cook over low heat for 8 minutes, or until soft. Add the garlic and cook for 30 seconds, then add the wine and simmer for 5 minutes.

3   Add the shanks, bay leaves, half the rosemary and 1.5 litres (52 fl oz/6 cups) of the stock to the pan. Season. Bring to the boil over high heat. Reduce the heat and simmer, covered, for 2 hours, or until the meat falls off the bone. Remove the shanks and cool slightly.

4   Take the meat off the bone and roughly chop. Add to the broth with the tomato, barley, the remaining rosemary and stock and simmer for 30 minutes. Add the vegetables and cook for 1 hour, or until the barley is tender. Remove the bay leaves, then stir in the redcurrant jelly.

GOULASH SOUP WITH DUMPLINGS

SERVES 4–6

3 tablespoons olive oil

1 kg (2 lb 4 oz) chuck or round steak, cut into 1 cm (½ inch) cubes

2 large onions, chopped

3 garlic cloves, crushed

1 green capsicum (pepper), chopped

1½ teaspoons caraway seeds, ground

3 tablespoons sweet paprika

¼ teaspoon ground nutmeg

pinch cayenne pepper

½ teaspoon sea salt

400 g (14 oz) tinned chopped tomatoes

2 litres (70 fl oz/8 cups) chicken stock

350 g (12 oz) potatoes, cut into 2 cm (¾ inch) cubes

1 green capsicum (pepper), julienned

2 tablespoons sour cream

DUMPLINGS

1 egg

3 tablespoons finely grated parmesan cheese

75 g (2½ oz/⅔ cup) self-raising flour

pinch cayenne pepper

1 Heat half the oil in a saucepan and brown the cubed beef in batches for 1–2 minutes. Remove and set aside. Heat the remaining oil in the same pan over low heat. Add the onion, garlic and chopped capsicum and cook for 5–6 minutes, or until softened. Stir in the spices and salt for 1 minute.

2 Return the beef to the pan and stir to coat. Stir in the tomato and stock and bring to the boil. Reduce the heat to low and simmer, covered, for 1¼ hours. Add the potato and cook for 30 minutes. Stir in the julienned capsicum and sour cream. Season.

3 To make the dumplings, mix together all the ingredients and a pinch of salt with a fork to form a soft dough (add 1–2 tablespoons water if necessary). Turn onto a lightly floured surface and knead for 5 minutes, or until smooth. Roll ½ teaspoonfuls of the dough into balls, drop into the simmering soup and cook for 6 minutes, or until cooked. Serve.

CHILLI CON CARNE SOUP

SERVES 4

1.25 litres (44 fl oz/5 cups) beef stock

1 tablespoon olive oil

1 onion, finely chopped

300 g (10½ oz) lean minced (ground) beef

1 garlic clove, crushed

3 teaspoons paprika

2 teaspoons cumin seeds

2 tablespoons tomato paste

440 g (14 oz) tinned red kidney beans, rinsed and drained

80 g (2¾ oz/⅓ cup) sour cream

1 **Pour the stock** into a saucepan and bring slowly to the boil over medium heat.

2 **Heat the oil** in a large heavy-based saucepan. Add the onion and cook, stirring, for 5 minutes, or until softened. Add the beef mince and cook until browned, breaking up any lumps with a fork. Stir in the garlic, paprika and cumin seeds and cook for a further 1 minute.

3 **Pour the stock** into the saucepan with the mince, then stir in the tomato paste and mix together well. Bring to the boil, then reduce the heat to low, add the drained kidney beans and simmer for 15 minutes, or until the soup has slightly thickened.

4 **Divide the soup** evenly among four warm soup bowls and top with a dollop of the sour cream. Season to taste with salt and freshly ground black pepper.

PROSCIUTTO, PEA AND POTATO SOUP

SERVES 4

1 tablespoon oil

1 onion, roughly chopped

4 prosciutto slices, roughly chopped

5 small potatoes, cut into 1 cm (½ inch) cubes

375 ml (13 fl oz/1½ cups) chicken stock

310 g (11 oz/2 cups) frozen peas

1 tablespoon shredded fresh sage leaves

1 Heat the oil in a saucepan and add the onion and prosciutto. Cook, stirring constantly, over high heat for 2–3 minutes, or until the onion is golden. Add the potato and cook for another minute.

2 Pour in the stock and 625 ml (21½ fl oz/2½ cups) water. Cook over medium heat for 15 minutes. Add the peas and cook for a further 5 minutes. Stir in the sage and season to taste with salt and freshly ground black pepper.

3 Divide the soup among four warm serving bowls. Serve with crusty bread and butter.

CHINESE BARBECUED PORK AND NOODLE SOUP

SERVES 4

1.25 litres (44 fl oz/5 cups) chicken stock

3 spring onions (scallions), cut into 4 cm (1½ inch) lengths

4 fresh ginger slices

1 tablespoon Chinese rice wine

1 tablespoon oyster sauce.

300 g (10½ oz) thinly sliced Chinese barbecued pork fillet

350 g (11 oz/2 cups) roughly chopped bok choy (pak choy)

200 g (7 oz) fresh flat egg noodles

sliced spring onion (scallion), to garnish

oyster sauce, to serve

1 Pour the stock and 250 ml (9 fl oz/1 cup) water into a large saucepan and bring to the boil, then reduce the heat to a simmer. Add the spring onion, ginger, Chinese rice wine and oyster sauce and simmer for 3–4 minutes before adding the pork. Continue to simmer for 4–5 minutes, then add the bok choy.

2 Meanwhile, bring a saucepan of lightly salted water to the boil and cook the noodles for 1 minute. Drain well and rinse under cold water, then divide the noodles among four deep bowls. When the bok choy is just wilted, remove it and the pork with a slotted spoon or tongs and divide evenly among the bowls. Cover with the broth. Sprinkle with a little spring onion, drizzle with some oyster sauce, then serve.

BEEF BALL AND WHITE BEAN SOUP

SERVES 4

600 g (1 lb 5 oz) minced (ground) beef

2 garlic cloves, crushed

1 tablespoon flat-leaf (Italian) parsley, finely chopped

large pinch ground cinnamon

large pinch freshly grated nutmeg

2 eggs, lightly beaten

1.5 litres (52 fl oz/6 cups) beef stock

2 carrots, thinly sliced

800 g (1 lb 12 oz) tinned white beans, drained

½ savoy cabbage, finely shredded

grated parmesan cheese, to serve

1 **Put the beef** in a bowl with the garlic, parsley, cinnamon, nutmeg and half of the egg. Mix to combine and season well. If the mixture is dry, add the rest of the egg—it needs to be sticky enough so that forming small balls is easy.

2 **Roll the beef** mixture into small balls—they should be small enough to scoop up on a spoon and eat in one mouthful.

3 **Put the beef stock** and the carrot in a saucepan and bring to the boil. Add the meatballs, one at a time, and reduce the heat. Simmer for 3 minutes. Add the beans and cabbage and cook for a further 4–5 minutes. Season to taste. Serve with grated parmesan.

CALDO GALLEGO

SERVES 4

250 g (9 oz/1¼ cups) white haricot beans, such as navy beans

500 g (1 lb 2 oz) smoked ham hock

2 tablespoons olive oil

1 leek, washed and chopped

1 garlic clove, chopped

500 g (1 lb 2 oz) pork babyback or American-style ribs separated into 5 cm (2 inch) widths

2 potatoes, peeled and cubed

1 bay leaf

1 kg (2 lb 4 oz) silverbeet (Swiss chard), washed well and chopped

1 Rinse the beans, then soak them in cold water for at least 5 hours. Put the ham hock in a large heavy-based saucepan and cover with cold water. Bring to the boil, then reduce the heat and simmer for about 1 hour, or until the meat starts to come away from the bone and is tender. Allow the hock to cool. When cool enough to handle, remove the meat from the bone and cut into 2 cm (¾ inch) cubes. Reserve 625 ml (22 fl oz/2½ cups) of the cooking liquid.

2 Meanwhile, put the beans in a large saucepan and cover with cold water. Bring to the boil, then reduce the heat and simmer for 30 minutes, or until tender. Drain, reserving 250 ml (9 fl oz/1 cup) of the cooking liquid.

3 Heat the olive oil in a large heavy-based saucepan over medium heat and cook the leek and garlic for about 5 minutes, or until translucent. Add the ham, beans, ribs, potato, bay leaf and reserved cups of cooking liquid (you need to make sure the food is covered with liquid).

4 Bring to the boil, then reduce the heat, cover and simmer for 45 minutes. Stir in the silverbeet and cook for a further 5 minutes. Season before serving

SPICY TOMATO SOUP WITH CHORIZO

SERVES 4–6

500 g (1 lb 2 oz) chorizo sausage

2 tablespoons olive oil

3 onions, halved and sliced

3 garlic cloves, thinly sliced

½ teaspoon ground cumin

1 teaspoon paprika

1–2 small red chillies, seeded and finely chopped

1.5 litres (52 fl oz/6 cups) chicken stock

800 g (1 lb 12 oz) tinned chopped tomatoes

4 tablespoons chopped flat-leaf (Italian) parsley

1 **Fill a large deep** frying pan with about 3 cm (1¼ inches) of cold water. Add the chorizo sausage, then bring to the boil over high heat. Reduce the heat and simmer, turning occasionally, for 15 minutes, or until the water evaporates, then continue to cook in any fat left in the pan for 3–4 minutes, or until the chorizo is lightly browned. Allow to cool slightly and break into bite-size pieces.

2 **Heat the oil** in a large saucepan over medium heat. Cook the onion and garlic for 5–6 minutes, or until soft. Stir in the cumin and paprika, chilli, chicken stock, tomato and half the parsley. Bring to the boil and add the chorizo. Reduce the heat and simmer for 20 minutes. Stir in the remaining parsley and serve immediately.

PORK CONGEE

SERVES 4–6

300 g (10½ oz/1½ cups) long-grain rice, thoroughly rinsed

½ star anise

2 spring onions (scallions), white part only

4 x 4 cm (1½ x 1½ inch) piece ginger, cut into slices

3.5 litres (118 fl oz/14 cups) chicken stock

1 tablespoon peanut oil

2 garlic cloves, crushed

1 teaspoon grated ginger, extra

400 g (14 oz) minced (ground) pork

ground white pepper

3 tablespoons light soy sauce

sesame oil, to drizzle

6 fried dough sticks (optional, see Note)

1   Put the rice in a large saucepan with the star anise, spring onions, sliced ginger and chicken stock. Bring to the boil, then reduce the heat to low and simmer for 1½ hours, stirring occasionally.

2   Heat the oil in a frying pan over high heat. Cook the garlic and grated ginger for 30 seconds. Add the pork and cook for 5 minutes, or until browned, breaking up any lumps with a spoon.

3   Remove the star anise, spring onions and ginger from the soup and discard. Add the pork mixture and simmer for 10 minutes. Season with white pepper and stir in the soy sauce. Serve with a drizzle of sesame oil and fried dough sticks, if desired.

Note: Fried dough sticks are available at Chinese bakeries and speciality shops and are best eaten soon after purchasing. If not, reheat in a 200°C (400°F/Gas 6) oven for 5 minutes, then serve.

LONG AND SHORT NOODLE SOUP

SERVES 6

300 g (10½ oz) minced (ground) pork

4 spring onions (scallions), sliced

3 garlic cloves, roughly chopped

2 teaspoons grated ginger

2 teaspoons cornflour (cornstarch)

125 ml (4 fl oz/½ cup) light soy sauce

3 tablespoons Chinese rice wine

30 won ton wrappers

3 litres (102 fl oz/12 cups) ready-made
  Chinese chicken broth, or home-
  made or ready-made chicken stock

200 g (7 oz) dried flat egg noodles

2 spring onions (scallions), extra, sliced
  on the diagonal

1 teaspoon sesame oil

1 Put the minced pork, spring onion, garlic, grated ginger, cornflour, 1½ tablespoons of the soy sauce and 1 tablespoon of the rice wine in a food processor and process until well combined. Place 2 teaspoons of the mixture in the centre of a won ton wrapper and lightly brush the edges with water. Lift the sides up tightly and pinch around the filling to form a pouch. Repeat this process to make 30 won tons.

2 Place the chicken broth in a large saucepan and bring to a simmer over medium–high heat. Stir in the remaining soy sauce and rice wine.

3 Meanwhile, bring a large pan of water to the boil. Reduce the heat, add the won tons and simmer for 1 minute, or until they float to the surface and are cooked through, then remove with a slotted spoon. Return the water to the boil, add the egg noodles and cook for 3 minutes, or until tender. Drain and add to the chicken broth along with the cooked won tons. Simmer for 2 minutes, or until heated through.

4 Divide the broth, noodles and won tons among six large serving bowls, sprinkle with extra spring onion and drizzle each with a little sesame oil.

SERVES 4

200 g (7 oz) rice noodle sticks

1.5 litres (52 fl oz/6 cups) beef stock

1 star anise

4 cm (1½ inch) piece fresh ginger, sliced

2 pigs trotters

½ onion, studded with 2 cloves

2 lemongrass stems, pounded

2 garlic cloves, pounded

¼ teaspoon white pepper

1 tablespoon fish sauce

400 g (14 oz) beef fillet, partially frozen, and thinly sliced

90 g (3¼ oz) bean sprouts, trimmed

2 spring onions (scallions), thinly sliced on the diagonal

25 g (1 oz) coriander (cilantro) leaves, chopped

25 g (1 oz) Vietnamese mint, chopped

1 fresh red chilli, thinly sliced

fresh red chillies, extra, to serve

Vietnamese mint, extra, to serve

coriander (cilantro) leaves, extra, to serve

2 limes, cut into quarters

fish sauce, extra, to serve

1 **Soak the noodles** in boiling water for 15–20 minutes. Drain well.

2 **Bring the stock,** star anise, ginger, trotters, onion, lemon grass, garlic and white pepper to the boil in a large saucepan. Reduce the heat and simmer for 30 minutes. Strain, return to the same pan and stir in the fish sauce.

3 **Divide the noodles** among bowls, then top with beef strips, sprouts, spring onion, coriander, mint and chilli. Ladle on the broth.

4 **Put the extra chilli,** mint, coriander, lime quarters and fish sauce in small bowls on a platter and serve with the soup.

SPICY LAMB SOUP

SERVES 4

2 large onions, roughly chopped

3 red chillies, seeded, chopped
(or 2 teaspoons dried chilli)

3–4 garlic cloves

2 cm (¾ inch) piece ginger, chopped

1 teaspoon ground black pepper

6 cm (2½ inch) lemongrass stem, white
only, chopped

½ teaspoon ground cardamom

2 teaspoons ground cumin

½ teaspoon ground cinnamon

1 teaspoon ground turmeric

2 tablespoons peanut oil

1.5 kg (3 lb 5 oz) lamb neck chops

2–3 tablespoons vindaloo paste

580 ml (20¼ fl oz/2⅓ cups) coconut
cream

45 g (1½ oz/¼ cup) soft brown sugar

2–3 tablespoons lime juice

4 kaffir lime leaves

1 Put the onion, chilli, garlic, ginger, pepper, lemon grass and spices in a food processor. Process to a paste. Heat half the oil in a large pan and brown the chops in batches. Remove.

2 Add the remaining oil to the pan and cook the spice and vindaloo pastes for 2–3 minutes. Add the chops and 1.75 litres (61 fl oz/7 cups) water, cover and bring to the boil. Reduce the heat; simmer, covered, for 1 hour. Remove the chops from the pan and stir in the coconut cream. Remove the meat from the bones, shred and return to the pan.

3 Add the sugar, lime juice and leaves. Simmer, uncovered, over low heat for 20–25 minutes, until slightly thickened. Garnish with coriander (cilantro).

BEEF AND CHILLI BEAN SOUP

SERVES 4

1 tablespoon oil

1 red onion, finely chopped

2 garlic cloves, crushed

2½ teaspoons chilli flakes

2½ teaspoons ground cumin

2½ tablespoons finely chopped coriander (cilantro) root and stem

1½ teaspoons ground coriander

500 g (1 lb 2 oz) lean minced (ground) beef

1 tablespoon tomato paste (concentrated purée)

4 tomatoes, peeled, seeded and diced

420 g (15 oz) tinned red kidney beans, drained and rinsed

2 litres (70 fl oz/8 cups) beef stock

3 tablespoons chopped coriander (cilantro) leaves

80 g (2¾ oz/⅓ cup) sour cream

1 Heat the oil in a large saucepan over medium heat. Cook the onion for about 2–3 minutes, or until softened. Add the garlic, chilli flakes, cumin, fresh and ground coriander, and cook for 1 minute. Add the beef and cook for 3–4 minutes, or until cooked through—break up any lumps with a spoon.

2 Add the tomato paste, tomato, beans and stock and bring to the boil. Reduce the heat and simmer for 15–20 minutes, or until reduced slightly. Remove any scum on the surface. Stir in the chopped coriander. Serve with sour cream.

POULTRY

TOM KHA GAI

SERVES 4

5 cm (2 inch) piece of fresh galangal or 5 slices of dried galangal

6 kaffir lime leaves

1 lemongrass stem, white part only, quartered

500 ml (17 fl oz/2 cups) coconut milk

500 ml (17 fl oz/2 cups) chicken stock

3 chicken breast fillets, cut into thin strips

1–2 teaspoons finely chopped red chillies

3 tablespoons lime juice

2 tablespoons fish sauce

1 teaspoon soft brown sugar

15 g (½ oz) coriander (cilantro) leaves

1 **Peel the galangal** and cut into thin slices. Mix the galangal, kaffir lime leaves and lemon grass with the coconut milk and stock in a medium pan. Bring to the boil, reduce the heat to low and simmer for 10 minutes, stirring occasionally.

2 **Add the chicken strips** and chilli and simmer for 8 minutes. Mix in the lime juice, fish sauce and sugar. Serve with the coriander leaves and garnish with coriander sprigs, if you want.

CHICKEN LAKSA

SERVES 4

CHICKEN BALLS

500 g (1 lb 2 oz) minced (ground)
  chicken

1 small red chilli, finely chopped

2 garlic cloves, finely chopped

½ small red onion, finely chopped

1 lemongrass stem, white part only,
  finely chopped

2 tablespoons chopped coriander
  (cilantro) leaves

200 g (7 oz) dried rice vermicelli

1 tablespoon peanut oil

75 g (2½ oz/¼ cup) good-quality laksa
  paste

1 litre (35 fl oz/4 cups) chicken stock

500 ml (17 fl oz/2 cups) coconut milk

8 fried tofu puffs, cut in half on
  the diagonal

90 g (3¼ oz) bean sprouts, trimmed

2 tablespoons shredded
  Vietnamese mint

3 tablespoons shredded coriander
  (cilantro) leaves

lime wedges, to serve

fish sauce, to serve (optional)

1   To make the balls, process all the ingredients in a food processor until just combined. Roll tablespoons of mixture into balls with wet hands.

2   Place the vermicelli in a heatproof bowl, cover with boiling water and soak for 6–7 minutes. Drain well.

3   Heat the oil in a large saucepan over medium heat. Add the laksa paste and cook for 1–2 minutes, or until aromatic. Add the stock, reduce the heat and simmer for 10 minutes. Add the coconut milk and the chicken balls and simmer for 5 minutes, or until the balls are cooked through.

4   Divide the vermicelli, tofu puffs and bean sprouts among four serving bowls and ladle the soup over the top, dividing the balls evenly. Garnish with the mint and coriander leaves. Serve with the lime wedges and, if desired, fish sauce.

CHICKEN, MUSHROOM AND MADEIRA SOUP

SERVES 4

10 g (¼ oz) dried porcini mushrooms

25 g (1 oz) butter

1 leek, white part only, thinly sliced

250 g (9 oz) pancetta, chopped

200 g (7 oz) Swiss brown mushrooms, roughly chopped

300 g (10½ oz) large field mushrooms, chopped

2 tablespoons plain (all-purpose) flour

125 ml (4 fl oz/½ cup) Madeira

1.25 litres (44 fl oz/5 cups) chicken stock

1 tablespoon olive oil

2 chicken breast fillets (about 200 g/ 7 oz each)

80 g (2¾ oz/⅓ cup) light sour cream

2 teaspoons chopped marjoram, plus whole leaves, to garnish

1 Soak the porcini in 250 ml (9 fl oz/1 cup) boiling water for 20 minutes.

2 Melt the butter in a large saucepan over medium heat and add the leek and pancetta. Cook for 5 minutes, or until the leek is softened. Add all the mushrooms and the porcini soaking liquid and cook for 10 minutes. Stir in the flour and cook for 1 minute. Add the Madeira and cook, stirring, for 10 minutes. Stir in the stock, bring to the boil, then reduce the heat and simmer for 45 minutes. Cool slightly.

3 Heat the oil in a frying pan and cook the chicken for 4–5 minutes each side, or until cooked through. Remove from the pan and thinly slice.

4 Blend the soup until smooth. Return to the saucepan, add the sour cream and chopped marjoram and stir over medium heat for about 1–2 minutes to warm through. Season. Top with the chicken and garnish with marjoram.

CREAMY CHICKEN AND CORN SOUP

SERVES 4–6

20 g (¾ oz) butter

1 tablespoon olive oil

500 g (1 lb 2 oz) chicken thigh fillets, trimmed and thinly sliced

2 garlic cloves, chopped

1 leek, chopped

1 large celery stalk, chopped

1 bay leaf

½ teaspoon thyme

1 litre (35 fl oz/4 cups) chicken stock

3 tablespoons sherry

550 g (1 lb 4 oz) corn kernels (fresh, canned or frozen)

1 large floury potato (russet), cut into 1 cm (½ inch) cubes

185 ml (6 fl oz/¾ cup) cream, plus extra, to drizzle

chives, to garnish

1 **Melt the butter** and oil in a large saucepan over high heat. Cook the chicken in batches for 3 minutes, or until lightly golden and just cooked through. Place in a bowl, cover and refrigerate until needed.

2 **Reduce the heat** to medium and stir in the garlic, leek, celery, bay leaf and thyme. Cook for 2 minutes, or until the leek softens—do not allow the garlic to burn. Add the stock, sherry and 500 ml (17 fl oz/2 cups) water and stir, scraping up any sediment stuck to the bottom of the pan. Add the corn and potato and bring to the boil. Reduce the heat and simmer for 1 hour, skimming any scum off the surface. Cool slightly.

3 **Remove the bay leaf** and purée the soup. Return to the cleaned pan, add the cream and chicken and stir over medium–low heat for 2–3 minutes, or until heated through— do not boil. Season. Drizzle with extra cream and garnish with chives. If desired, serve with crusty bread.

DUCK, MUSHROOMS AND RICE NOODLE BROTH

SERVES 4–6

3 dried shiitake mushrooms

1 Chinese roast duck (1.5 kg/3 lb 5 oz)

500 ml (17 fl oz/2 cups) chicken stock

2 tablespoons light soy sauce

1 tablespoon Chinese rice wine

2 teaspoons sugar

400 g (14 oz) fresh flat rice noodles

2 tablespoons oil

3 spring onions (scallions), thinly sliced

1 teaspoon finely chopped ginger

400 g (14 oz) bok choy (pak choy),
  trimmed and leaves separated

¼ teaspoon sesame oil

1 Place the shiitake mushrooms in a heatproof bowl, cover with 250 ml (9 fl oz/1 cup) boiling water and soak for 20 minutes. Drain, reserving the liquid and squeezing the excess liquid from the mushrooms. Discard the woody stems and thinly slice the caps.

2 Remove the skin and flesh from the roast duck. Discard the fat and carcass. Finely slice the duck meat and the skin.

3 Place the chicken stock, soy sauce, rice wine, sugar and the reserved mushroom liquid in a saucepan over medium heat. Bring to a simmer and cook for 5 minutes. Meanwhile, place the rice noodles in a heatproof bowl, cover with boiling water and soak briefly. Gently separate the noodles with your hands and drain well. Divide evenly among large soup bowls.

4 Heat the oil in a wok over high heat. Add the spring onion, ginger and shiitake mushrooms and cook for several seconds. Transfer to the broth with the bok choy and duck meat and simmer for 1 minute, or until the duck has warmed through and the bok choy has wilted. Ladle the soup over the noodles and drizzle sesame oil on each serving. Serve immediately.

SERVES 4

1 carrot, chopped

1 large leek, chopped

2 bay leaves

2 chicken breast fillets

2 litres (70 fl oz/8 cups) chicken stock

75 g (2½ oz/⅓ cup) short-grain rice

3 eggs, separated

4 tablespoons lemon juice

2 tablespoons chopped parsley

40 g (1½ oz) butter, chopped

1 **Place the carrot**, leek, bay leaves, chicken fillets and stock in a large saucepan. Bring to the boil over high heat, then reduce the heat and simmer for 10–15 minutes, or until the chicken is cooked. Strain into a clean saucepan and reserve the chicken.

2 **Add the rice** to the liquid, bring to the boil, then reduce the heat and simmer for 15 minutes, or until tender. Cut the chicken into 1 cm (½ inch) cubes.

3 **Whisk the egg whites** in a clean, dry bowl until firm peaks form. Beat in the yolks until light and creamy, whisk in the lemon juice, then 250 ml (9 fl oz/1 cup) of the soup. Remove the soup from the heat and gradually whisk in the egg mixture. Add the chicken and stir over low heat for 2 minutes — do not boil or the egg will scramble. Serve at once with a sprinkle of parsley and dot of butter.

Note: This soup will not stand well — make just before serving.

CHICKEN AND VEGETABLE SOUP

SERVES 4–6

1.5 kg (3 lb 5 oz) chicken

1 onion

2 large leeks, halved lengthwise and well washed

3 large celery stalks

5 black peppercorns

1 bay leaf

2 large carrots, peeled and diced

1 large swede (rutabaga), peeled and diced

2 large tomatoes, peeled, seeded and finely chopped

165 g (5¾ oz/¾ cup) barley

1 tablespoon tomato paste (purée)

2 tablespoons finely chopped flat-leaf (Italian) parsley

1 Put the chicken, onion, 1 leek, 1 celery stalk, halved, the peppercorns and bay leaf in a large saucepan and add enough water to cover. Bring to the boil, then reduce the heat and simmer for 1½ hours, skimming any impurities that rise to the surface.

2 Strain the stock through a fine sieve and return to the cleaned saucepan. Discard the onion, leek, celery, peppercorns and bay leaf, and set the chicken aside. When it is cool enough to handle, discard the fat and bones, then shred the flesh, cover and chill.

3 Allow the stock to cool, then refrigerate overnight. Skim the fat from the surface, place the stock in a large saucepan and bring to the boil. Dice the remaining leek and celery and add to the soup with the carrot, swede, tomato, barley and tomato paste. Simmer for 45–50 minutes, or until the vegetables are cooked and the barley is tender. Stir in the parsley and shredded chicken. Simmer until warmed through and season.

CREAMY CHICKEN AND PAPRIKA SOUP

SERVES 4–6

90 g (3¼ oz) butter
1 onion, finely chopped
1 stick celery, finely chopped
1 small carrot, finely chopped
2 tablespoons Hungarian sweet paprika
40 g (1½ oz/⅓ cup) plain (all-purpose) flour
2 litres (70 fl oz/8 cups) chicken stock
125 ml (4 fl oz/½ cup) cream (whipping)
300 g (10½ oz) boneless, skinless cooked chicken breasts, finely chopped
crusty bread, to serve

1 In a large saucepan, melt the butter over medium–high heat. Add the onion, celery and carrot and cook for 5 minutes, or until the vegetables have softened.

2 Add the paprika and cook for 1 minute, or until the paprika becomes fragrant. Quickly toss in the flour and stir until well combined. Cook for a further 1 minute and remove from the heat.

3 Add one-third of the stock and mix to a thick paste, stirring out all the lumps. Return the pan to the heat and add the remaining stock. Stir until the soup boils and thickens slightly. Reduce the heat, cover and simmer for 45–50 minutes.

4 Remove the soup from the heat and stir in the cream and chicken. Season to taste and serve with crusty bread.

CREAMY BROCCOLI AND CHICKEN SOUP

SERVES 4

1 tablespoon oil

2 garlic cloves, crushed

4 spring onions (scallions), sliced

1 litre (35 fl oz/1 cup) chicken stock

500 g (1 lb 2 oz) broccoli florets

400 g (14 oz) chicken breast fillets, cut into thin strips

125 g (4½ oz/½ cup) sour cream

1 **Heat the oil in a saucepan.** Add the garlic and spring onion and cook over medium heat for 1–2 minutes, or until softened.

2 **Add the stock,** bring to the boil, then reduce the heat and simmer. Add the broccoli to the stock and cook, covered, over low heat, for 3–5 minutes, or until the broccoli is tender but still green.

3 **Transfer the soup** to a blender or food processor and blend in batches until completely smooth.

4 **Return to the pan** and bring to the boil. Add the chicken strips, reduce the heat and simmer for 3–5 minutes, or until the chicken is cooked. Add the sour cream and season with salt and pepper. Reheat gently just before serving.

CHICKEN AND SPINACH RISONI SOUP

SERVES 4

1 tablespoon olive oil

1 leek, quartered lengthways and thinly sliced

2 garlic cloves, crushed

1 teaspoon ground cumin

1.5 litres (52 fl oz/6 cups) chicken stock

2 boneless, skinless chicken breast fillets

205 g (7¼ oz/1 cup) risoni

150 g (5½ oz) baby English spinach leaves, roughly chopped

1 tablespoon chopped dill

2 teaspoons lemon juice

1   Heat the oil in a large saucepan over low heat. Add the leek and cook for about 8–10 minutes, or until soft. Add the garlic and cumin and cook for 1 minute. Pour the stock into the pan, increase the heat to high and bring to the boil. Reduce the heat to low, add the chicken fillets and simmer, covered, for 8 minutes. Remove the chicken from the broth, allow to cool slightly, then shred.

2   Stir the risoni into the broth and simmer for 12 minutes, or until al dente.

3   Return the chicken to the broth along with the spinach and dill. Simmer for 2 minutes, or until the spinach has wilted. Stir in the lemon juice and season to taste.

FIVE-SPICE DUCK AND SOMEN NOODLE SOUP

SERVES 4

4 duck breasts, skin on

1 teaspoon Chinese five-spice

1 teaspoon peanut oil

200 g (7 oz) dried somen noodles

STAR ANISE BROTH

1 litre (35 fl oz/4 cups) chicken stock

3 whole star anise

5 spring onions (scallions), chopped

1 large handful coriander (cilantro)
  leaves, chopped

1 **Preheat the oven** to 200°C (400°F/Gas 6). Trim the duck breast of excess fat, then lightly sprinkle both sides with the Chinese five-spice.

2 **Heat the oil** in a large frying pan over medium heat. Add the duck, skin side down, and cook for 2–3 minutes, or until brown and crisp. Turn and cook the other side for 3 minutes. Transfer to a baking tray and cook, skin side up, for a further 8–10 minutes, or until cooked to your liking.

3 **Meanwhile,** put the chicken stock and star anise in a small saucepan. Bring to the boil, then reduce the heat and simmer for 5 minutes. Add the spring onion and coriander and simmer for 5 minutes.

4 **Cook the noodles** in a saucepan of boiling water for 2 minutes, or until soft. Drain and divide among four bowls. Ladle the broth on the noodles and top each bowl with one sliced duck breast.

EIGHT TREASURE NOODLE SOUP

SERVES 4

10 g (¼ oz) dried shiitake mushrooms

375 g (13 oz) thick fresh egg noodles

1.25 litres (44 fl oz/5 cups) chicken stock

3 tablespoons light soy sauce

2 teaspoons Chinese rice wine

200 g (7 oz) chicken breast fillet, cut into 1 cm (½ inch) strips on the diagonal

200 g (7 oz) Chinese barbecued pork (char sui), cut into 5 mm (¼ inch) slices

¼ onion, finely chopped

1 carrot, cut into 1 cm (½ inch) slices on the diagonal

125 g (4½ oz) snow peas (mangetout), cut in half on the diagonal

4 spring onions (scallions), thinly sliced

1 Place the shiitake mushrooms in a heatproof bowl, cover with boiling water and soak for 20 minutes, or until soft. Drain and squeeze out any excess liquid. Discard the woody stems and thinly slice the caps.

2 Bring a large saucepan of water to the boil and cook the noodles for 1 minute, or until cooked through. Drain, then rinse with cold water. Divide evenly into four deep warmed serving bowls.

3 Meanwhile, bring the chicken stock to the boil in a large saucepan over high heat. Reduce the heat to medium and add the soy sauce and rice wine, stirring to combine. Simmer for 2 minutes. Add the chicken and pork and cook for another 2 minutes, or until the chicken is cooked through and the pork is heated. Add the onion, carrot, snow peas, shiitake mushrooms and half the spring onion and cook for a further 1 minute, or until the carrot is tender.

4 Divide the vegetables and meat among the serving bowls and ladle on the hot broth. Garnish each bowl with the remaining spring onion.

SPICY PORTUGUESE CHICKEN SOUP

SERVES 6

2.5 litres (85 fl oz/10 cups) chicken stock

1 onion, cut into thin wedges

1 celery stalk, finely chopped

1 teaspoon grated lemon zest

3 tomatoes, peeled, seeded and chopped

1 mint sprig

1 tablespoon olive oil

2 chicken breast fillets

200 g (7 oz/1 cup) long-grain rice

2 tablespoons lemon juice

2 tablespoons shredded mint

1 **Combine the chicken stock,** onion, celery, lemon zest, tomatoes, mint and olive oil in a large saucepan. Slowly bring to the boil, then reduce the heat, add the chicken and simmer gently for 20–25 minutes, or until the chicken is cooked through.

2 **Remove the chicken** from the saucepan and discard the mint sprig. Allow the chicken to cool, then thinly slice.

3 **Meanwhile,** add the rice to the pan and simmer for 25–30 minutes, or until the rice is tender. Return the sliced chicken to the pan, add the lemon juice and stir for 1–2 minutes, or until the chicken is warmed through. Season and stir through the mint.

DUCK, SHIITAKE MUSHROOMS AND RICE NOODLE BROTH

SERVES 4–6

1 whole Chinese roast duck

4 coriander (cilantro) roots and stems, well rinsed

5 slices fresh galangal

4 spring onions (scallions), sliced on the diagonal into 3 cm (1¼ inch) lengths

400 g (14 oz) Chinese broccoli (gai larn), cut into 5 cm (2 inch) lengths

2 garlic cloves, crushed

3 tablespoons fish sauce

1 tablespoon hoisin sauce

2 teaspoons grated palm sugar or soft brown sugar

½ teaspoon ground white pepper

500 g (1 lb 2 oz) fresh rice noodles

crispy fried garlic flakes, to garnish (optional)

coriander (cilantro) leaves, to garnish (optional)

1 **To make the stock,** cut off the duck's head and discard. Remove the skin and fat, leaving the neck intact. Remove the flesh from the bones and set aside. Cut any fat from the carcass along with the parson's nose, then discard. Break the carcass into pieces, then put in a stockpot with 2 litres (70 fl oz/8 cups) of water.

2 **Bruise the coriander roots** and stems with the back of a knife. Add to the pot with the galangal and bring to the boil. Skim off any foam from the surface. Boil over medium heat for 15 minutes. Strain the stock through a fine sieve, discard the carcass, and return the stock to a clean saucepan.

3 **Slice the duck flesh** into strips. Add to the stock with the spring onion, Chinese broccoli, garlic, fish sauce, hoisin sauce, palm sugar and white pepper. Gently bring to the boil.

4 **Cook the noodles** in boiling water for 2–3 minutes, or until tender. Drain well. Divide the noodles and soup evenly among the serving bowls. If desired, garnish with the garlic flakes and coriander leaves.

CHICKEN AND PUMPKIN LAKSA

SERVES 4

2 bird's eye chillies, chopped

2 lemongrass stems, white part only, chopped

4 red Asian shallots, peeled

1 tablespoon chopped ginger

1 teaspoon ground turmeric

3 candlenuts (optional)

110 g (3¾ oz) dried rice noodle sticks

1 tablespoon peanut oil

250 g (9 oz) butternut pumpkin (squash), cut into chunks

800 ml (28 fl oz) coconut milk

600 g (1 lb 5 oz) chicken breast fillets, cut into cubes

2 tablespoons lime juice

1 tablespoon fish sauce

90 g (3¼ oz) bean sprouts, trimmed

15 g (½ oz) torn basil

10 g (¼ oz) torn mint

50 g (1¾ oz/½ cup) unsalted peanuts, toasted and chopped

1 lime, cut into quarters

1   Put all the paste ingredients in a food processor with 1 tablespoon of water and blend until smooth.

2   Soak the noodles in boiling water for 15–20 minutes. Drain well.

3   Meanwhile, heat the oil in a wok and swirl to coat. Add the paste and stir over low heat for 5 minutes, or until aromatic. Add the pumpkin and coconut milk and simmer for 10 minutes. Add the chicken and simmer for 20 minutes. Stir in the lime juice and fish sauce.

4   Divide the noodles among four deep serving bowls, then ladle the soup over them. Top with the bean sprouts, basil, mint, peanuts and lime.

CURRIED CHICKEN NOODLE SOUP

SERVES 4

175 g (6 oz) dried thin egg noodles

2 tablespoons peanut oil

2 chicken breasts (about 250 g/9 oz each)

1 onion, sliced

1 small fresh red chilli, seeded and finely chopped

1 tablespoon finely chopped fresh ginger

2 tablespoons Indian curry powder

750 ml (26 fl oz/3 cups) chicken stock

800 ml (28 fl oz) coconut milk

300 g (10½ oz) baby bok choy (pak choy), cut into long strips

20 g (¾ oz) basil, torn

1 Cook the noodles in a large saucepan of boiling water for 3-4 minutes, or until cooked. Drain well and set aside. Wipe the sauce pan clean and dry.

2 Heat the oil in the dry pan and add the chicken. Cook on each side for 5 minutes, or until cooked through. Remove the chicken and keep warm. **Place the onion** in the pan and cook over low heat for 8 minutes, or until softened but not browned. Add the chilli, ginger and curry powder and cook for a further 2 minutes. Add the chicken stock and bring to the boil. Reduce the heat and simmer for 20 minutes. Thinly slice the chicken on the diagonal.

3 Add the coconut milk to the saucepan and simmer for 10 minutes. Add the bok choy and cook for 3 minutes, then stir in the basil.

4 To serve, divide the noodles among four deep serving bowls. Top with slices of chicken and ladle in the soup. Serve immediately.

LEMON CHICKEN SOUP

SERVES 4

2 chicken breast fillets

1 lemon

1 litre (35 fl oz/4 cups) chicken stock (see Note)

2 fresh lemon thyme sprigs, plus extra, to serve (see Note)

1 **Trim any excess** fat from the chicken. Using a vegetable peeler, cut 2 strips of rind from the lemon and remove the pith. Place the stock, rind and lemon thyme in a shallow pan and slowly bring almost to the boil. Reduce to simmering point, add the chicken and cook, covered, for 7 minutes, or until the meat is tender.

2 **Remove the chicken** from the pan, transfer to a plate and cover with foil.

3 **Strain the stock** into a clean pan through a sieve lined with 2 layers of damp muslin. Finely shred the chicken and return to the soup. Reheat gently and season to taste with salt and freshly ground black pepper. Serve immediately, garnished with the extra sprigs of lemon thyme.

Note: If you don't have time to make your own stock, poultry shops or butchers sometimes sell their own. These may have more flavour and contain less salt than stock cubes. You can use ordinary thyme if lemon thyme is not available.

JUNGLE SOUP

SERVES 4

2 teaspoons oil
1 onion, finely sliced
225 g (8 oz) butternut pumpkin (squash), peeled and diced
225 g (8 oz) pineapple or mango, chopped
1 garlic clove, crushed
1 dried red chilli, finely chopped
2 teaspoons grated ginger
1 litre (35 fl oz/4 cups) chicken stock
2 tablespoons lime juice
350 g (12 oz) chicken breast, cut diagonally into thin strips

1 **Heat the oil** in a large heavy-based pan and cook the onion for 5 minutes, or until golden. Add the pumpkin and cook for 5 minutes, or until just brown. Add the pineapple, garlic, chilli and ginger and toss together.

2 **Add the stock** and lime juice, bring to the boil and then reduce the heat to simmer for 20 minutes, or until the pumpkin is nearly tender.

3 **Add the chicken** and simmer for 5 minutes, or until the chicken is cooked. Serve immediately.

SEAFOOD

BOURRIDE

SERVES 4

GARLIC CROUTONS
½ stale baguette, sliced

60 ml (2 fl oz/¼ cup) olive oil

1 garlic clove, halved

AIOLI
2 egg yolks

4 garlic cloves, crushed

4 teaspoons lemon juice

250 ml (9 fl oz/1 cup) olive oil

STOCK
¼ teaspoon dry saffron threads

1 litre (35 fl oz/4 cups) white wine

1 leek, white part only,

2 carrots, chopped

2 onions, chopped

2 long pieces orange zest, chopped

2 teaspoons fennel seeds

3 thyme sprigs

2.5 kg (5 lb 8 oz) whole firm white
fish such as monkfish, sea bass, cod,
perch, sole or bream, filleted, skinned
and cut into 4 cm pieces (reserve the
trimmings)

3 egg yolks

1 Preheat the oven to 160°C (315°F/Gas 2–3). Brush the bread with oil and bake for 10 minutes until crisp. Rub one side of each slice with garlic.

2 To make the aioli, put the egg yolks, garlic and 3 teaspoons of the lemon juice in a mortar and pestle or food processor and pound or mix until light and creamy. Add the oil, drop by drop from the tip of a teaspoon, whisking constantly until it begins to thicken, then add the oil in a very thin stream. Season, add the remaining lemon juice and, if necessary, thin with a little warm water. Cover and refrigerate.

3 To make the stock, soak the saffron in a tablespoon of hot water for 15 minutes. Put the saffron, wine, leek, carrot, onion, orange zest, fennel seeds, thyme and fish trimmings in a large saucepan with 1 litre water. Cover and bring to the boil, then simmer for 20 minutes, skimming occasionally. Strain into a

clean saucepan, pressing the solids with a wooden spoon to extract all the liquid. Bring the stock to a gentle simmer, add half the fish and poach for 5 minutes. Remove and keep warm while you cook the rest of the fish, then remove them from the pan and bring the stock back to the boil. Boil for 5 minutes, or until slightly reduced, and remove from the heat.

4 Put half the aioli and the yolks in a bowl and mix until smooth. Whisk in a ladleful of hot stock, then gradually add 5 ladlefuls, stirring constantly. Pour back into the pan holding the rest of the stock and whisk over low heat for 3–5 minutes, or until the soup is hot and slightly thicker (don't let it boil or it will curdle). Season with salt and pepper.

5 To serve, put two garlic croutons in each bowl, top with a few pieces of fish and ladle over the hot soup. Serve the remaining aioli separately.

SERVES 4

300 g (10½ oz) red mullet fillets

400 g (14 oz) firm white fish fillets

300 g (10½ oz) calamari, cleaned

1.5 litres (52 fl oz/6 cups) fish stock

80 ml (2½ fl oz/⅓ cup) olive oil

1 onion, chopped

6 garlic cloves, chopped

1 small red chilli, chopped

1 teaspoon sweet pimentón (paprika)

a pinch saffron threads

150 ml (5 fl oz) white wine

400 g (14 oz) tinned crushed tomatoes

16 raw prawns (shrimp), peeled and
deveined, tails intact

2 tablespoons brandy

24 debearded and scrubbed black
mussels

1 tablespoon flat-leaf (Italian) parsley
chopped, to garnish

PICADA

2 tablespoons olive oil

2 slices day-old bread, diced

2 garlic cloves

5 blanched almonds, roasted

2 tablespoons flat-leaf (Italian) parsley

1 Cut the fish and calamari into 4 cm (1½ inch) pieces. Pour the stock into a large saucepan, bring to the boil and heat for about 20 minutes, or until reduced by half.

2 To make the picada, heat the olive oil in a frying pan, add the bread and stir for 3 minutes, or until golden, adding the garlic for the last minute. Process the bread, garlic, almonds and parsley in a food processor. Add enough stock to make a smooth paste.

3 Heat 2 tablespoons of the oil in a large saucepan, add the onion, garlic, chilli and paprika, and cook, stirring, for 1 minute. Add the saffron, white wine, tomato and stock. Bring to the boil, then reduce the heat and leave to simmer.

4 Heat the remaining oil in another frying pan over medium heat and cook the fish and calamari for 3–5 minutes. Remove from the pan. Add the prawns, cook for 1 minute, then add the brandy. Carefully ignite the brandy and let the flames burn down. Remove the prawns from the pan.

5 Add the mussels to the hot stock and simmer, covered, for about 3 minutes, or until opened. Discard any that do not open. Return all the seafood to the saucepan, add the picada, and stir until the sauce has thickened slightly and the seafood is cooked. Season to taste. Serve garnished with parsley.

LAKSA LEMAK

SERVES 4

115 g (4 oz) rice noodles

50 g (1¾ oz) unsalted macadamias

1 tablespoon oil

800 ml (28 fl oz) canned coconut milk

80 ml (2½ fl oz/⅓ cup) lime juice

115 g (4 oz) bean sprouts, trimmed

20 large raw prawns (shrimp), peeled and deveined

16 large scallops, cleaned

a handful of Vietnamese mint, shredded, a few leaves left whole to garnish

½ Lebanese (short) cucumber, peeled and thinly sliced

PASTE

3 red chillies, seeded and chopped

2 lemon grass stems

a small knob fresh ginger, grated

4 red Asian shallots, peeled

3 teaspoons shrimp paste

3 teaspoons ground turmeric

1 Soak the rice noodles in boiling water for 10 minutes. Drain.

2 To make the paste, put all the paste ingredients, plus 1 tablespoon water, into a food processor and blend until smooth. Alternatively, finely chop by hand and mix well.

3 Put the nuts in a saucepan and dry-roast over medium heat, shaking the pan, until golden. Transfer to a plate.

4 Heat the oil in the same saucepan, add the prepared paste and cook over medium heat for 2 minutes. Stir in the coconut milk, then gently simmer for 10 minutes, or until it thickens slightly. Roughly chop the nuts.

5 When the coconut milk mixture is ready, add the lime juice and three-quarters of the bean sprouts to the pan. Season with salt, bring back to a simmer, then add the prawns and scallops and cook for about 5 minutes, or until the prawns have turned pink. Add the shredded mint and the noodles. Mix the whole mint leaves with the chopped nuts and cucumber.

6 Ladle into 4 deep bowls, then sprinkle with the remaining bean sprouts and the mint and cucumber mixture.

SMOKED FISH CHOWDER

500 ml (17 fl oz/2 cups) milk
500 g (1 lb 2 oz) smoked fish, trimmed and cut into large chunks
50 g (1¾ oz) butter
1 leek, white part only, roughly chopped
2 celery stalks, chopped
1 large carrot, chopped
2 garlic cloves, chopped
3 potatoes (about 400 g/14 oz), cut into 5 cm (2 inch) pieces
1 teaspoon freshly grated nutmeg
500 ml (17 fl oz/2 cups) fish stock
125 ml (4 fl oz/½ cup) cream
1 large handful flat-leaf (Italian) parsley, chopped

1 Heat the milk in a large deep saucepan. Add the fish and simmer for 8 minutes, or until the flesh flakes when tested. Transfer the fish to a plate and set aside to cool. Reserve the milk. Peel and discard the skin from the fish and roughly flake the flesh, removing any bones.

2 Heat the butter in a large heavy-based saucepan over medium–low heat. Add the leek, celery, carrot and garlic. Stir for 2 minutes to coat the vegetables in the butter. Reduce the heat, cover and sweat, stirring occasionally, for 5 minutes. Do not allow the vegetables to brown.

3 Add the chopped potato and nutmeg to the saucepan and stir to combine. Cook for 2 minutes, then add the stock. Bring to the boil, cover and cook for 20 minutes, or until the potato is tender. Set aside to cool slightly.

4 Using an immersion blender fitted with the chopping blade, whizz the soup for 10 seconds, or until roughly puréed. Stir in the fish, reserved milk, cream and parsley and gently reheat the soup. Season well with freshly ground black pepper.

Note: The soup will keep in the refrigerator, covered, for up to 3 days. It is not suitable for freezing.

POTATO AND ANCHOVY CHOWDER WITH PRAWNS

SERVES 4

GARLIC PRAWNS

2 garlic cloves, chopped

1 small red chilli, seeded and chopped

2 tablespoons chopped flat-leaf (Italian) parsley

1 tablespoon olive oil

16 raw prawns (shrimp), peeled and deveined

1 tablespoon olive oil

3 bacon slices, fat trimmed, chopped

1 onion, chopped

2 celery stalks, chopped

2 garlic cloves, chopped

80 g (2¾ oz) tinned anchovies, drained

1 carrot, chopped

3 potatoes, about 400 g (14 oz), roughly chopped

375 ml (13 fl oz/1½ cups) chicken stock or fish stock

250 ml (9 fl oz/1 cup) milk

125 ml (4 fl oz/½ cup) cream

3 tablespoons finely chopped flat-leaf (Italian) parsley

1 To make the garlic prawns, put the garlic, chilli and parsley in a mini processor and whizz for 15–20 seconds, or until finely chopped. With the motor running, add the oil and continue whizzing until the mixture forms a rough paste. Transfer to a bowl, add the prawns and toss to coat. Set aside to marinate for 30 minutes.

2 Heat the oil in a large heavy-based saucepan over medium–low heat. Add the bacon, onion, celery and garlic and cook, stirring, for 2 minutes. Reduce the heat, cover and simmer, stirring occasionally, for 5 minutes. Do not allow the bacon and vegetables to brown.

3 Drain the anchovies on paper towels and pat dry. Roughly chop and add to the bacon mixture. Add the carrot and potato and stir to combine. Cook for 2 minutes, then add the stock and milk. Bring to the boil, then cover and cook for 15 minutes, or until the vegetables are tender.

4 Remove the saucepan from the heat. Using an immersion blender fitted with the chopping blade, whizz the soup for 20–30 seconds, or until smooth. Add the cream and most of the parsley, reserving some for garnishing. Season well with freshly ground black pepper and keep warm.

5 Heat a large frying pan over high heat and add the prawns and marinade all at once. Cook, turning, for 2 minutes, or until the prawns are just cooked through.

6 Place a pile of prawns in the centre of four large soup bowls and ladle the soup around the prawns. Sprinkle with the remaining parsley and serve immediately.

GREAT TASTES SOUPS

PRAWN GUMBO

SERVES 4

2 tablespoons olive oil

1 large onion, finely chopped

3 garlic cloves, crushed

1 red capsicum (pepper), chopped

4 bacon slices, chopped

1½ teaspoons dried thyme

2 teaspoons dried oregano

1 teaspoon paprika

½ teaspoon cayenne pepper

3 tablespoons sherry

1 litre (35 fl oz/4 cups) fish stock

100 g (3½ oz/½ cup) long-grain rice

2 bay leaves

400 g (14 oz) tinned chopped tomatoes

150 g (5½ oz) okra, thinly sliced

850 g (1 lb 14 oz) raw prawns (shrimp), peeled and deveined

3 tablespoons finely chopped flat-leaf (Italian) parsley

1 **Heat the oil** in a large saucepan over low heat. Cook the onion, garlic, capsicum and bacon for 5 minutes, or until soft. Stir in the herbs and spices. Season. Add the sherry and cook until evaporated, then add the stock and 500 ml (17 fl oz/ 2 cups) water. Bring to the boil. Add the rice and bay leaves, reduce the heat and simmer, covered, for 20 minutes.

2 **Add the tomato** and okra. Simmer, covered, for 20–25 minutes. Stir in the prawns and parsley and simmer for 5 minutes, or until the prawns are cooked through.

SPICY SEAFOOD AND ROASTED CORN SOUP

SERVES 4

2 corn cobs (700 g/1 lb 9 oz)

1 tablespoon olive oil

1 red onion, finely chopped

1 small red chilli, finely chopped

½ teaspoon ground allspice

4 vine-ripened tomatoes, peeled and finely diced

1.5 litres (52 fl oz/6 cups) fish stock or light chicken stock

300 g (10½ oz) boneless firm white fish fillets, diced

200 g (7 oz) fresh crabmeat

200 g (7 oz) peeled raw prawns (shrimp), roughly chopped

1 tablespoon lime juice

QUESADILLAS

4 flour tortillas (19 cm/7½ inch)

85 g (3 oz/⅔ cup) grated cheddar cheese

1 large handful coriander (cilantro) leaves

2 tablespoons olive oil

1 **Preheat the oven** to 200°C (400°F/Gas 6). Peel back the husks on the corn cobs and remove the silks. Fold the husks back over the corn, put in a baking dish and bake for 1 hour, or until the corn is tender.

2 **Heat the oil** in a saucepan over medium heat. Add the onion and cook until soft. Add the chilli and allspice and cook for 1 minute, then add the tomato and stock and bring to the boil. Reduce the heat and simmer, covered, for 45 minutes. Slice off the kernels from the corn cobs, add to the soup and simmer for 15 minutes. Add the fish, crab and prawn meat and simmer for 5 minutes. Add the lime juice.

3 **Meanwhile,** to make the quesadillas, top one tortilla with half the cheese and half the coriander. Season, then top with another tortilla. Heat 1 tablespoon of the oil in a frying pan and cook the quesadilla for 30 seconds on each side. Repeat. Cut into wedges and serve with the soup.

POACHED SEAFOOD BROTH WITH SOBA NOODLES

SERVES 4

250 g (9 oz) dried soba noodles

8 raw prawns (shrimp)

1½ tablespoons finely chopped ginger

4 spring onions (scallions), cut on the diagonal

100 ml (3½ fl oz) light soy sauce

3 tablespoons mirin

1 teaspoon grated palm sugar or soft brown sugar

300 g (10½ oz) boneless salmon fillet, skinned and cut into 5 cm (2 inch) strips

300 g (10½ oz) boneless white fish fillet, skinned and cut into 5 cm (2 inch) strips

150 g (5½ oz) cleaned calamari hood, scored and cut into 3 cm (1¼ inch) cubes

50 g (1¾ oz) mizuna, roughly chopped (see Note)

1 Cook the noodles in a large saucepan of boiling water for 5 minutes, or until tender. Drain and rinse with cold water.

2 Peel and devein the prawns, reserving the shells and leaving the tails intact. Place the heads and shells in a large saucepan with the ginger, half the spring onion and 1.5 litres (52 fl oz/6 cups) water. Bring slowly to the boil and boil for 5 minutes. Strain and discard the prawn heads, shells and spring onion. Return the stock to the pan. Add the soy sauce, mirin and palm sugar to the stock. Heat and stir to dissolve the sugar.

3 Add the seafood to the pan and poach over low heat for 2–3 minutes, or until it is just cooked. Add the remaining spring onion.

4 Divide the noodles evenly among four large bowls. Add the seafood, pour on the stock and scatter with the mizuna.

Note: Mizuna is a salad leaf with dark green, feathery and glossy leaves. It has a mild peppery flavour. Young leaves are often used in salads or as a garnish, while older leaves are used in stir-fries or in Japanese cooking.

CRAB BISQUE

SERVES 4

50 g (1¾ oz) butter

½ carrot, finely chopped

½ onion, finely chopped

1 celery stalk, finely chopped

1 bay leaf

2 thyme sprigs

1 kg (2 lb 4 oz) live crabs, cleaned and claws detached

2 tablespoons tomato paste (concentrated purée)

2 tablespoons brandy

150 ml (5 fl oz) dry white wine

1 litre (35 fl oz/4 cups) fish stock

60 g (2¼ oz) rice

3 tablespoons thick cream

¼ teaspoon cayenne pepper

1 **Heat the butter** in a large saucepan. Add the vegetables, bay leaf and thyme and cook over medium heat for 3 minutes, without allowing the vegetables to colour. Add the crab claws, legs and bodies and cook for 5 minutes, or until the crab shells turn red. Add the tomato paste, brandy and white wine and simmer for 2 minutes, or until reduced by half.

2 **Add the stock** and 500 ml (17 fl oz/2 cups) of water and bring to the boil. Reduce the heat and simmer for 5 minutes. Remove the shells, leaving the crab meat in the stock, and reserve the claws to use as a garnish. Finely crush the shells in a mortar and pestle (or in a food processor with a little of the stock).

3 **Return the crushed shells** to the soup with the rice. Bring to the boil, reduce the heat, cover and simmer for about 20 minutes, or until the rice is soft.

4 **Immediately** strain the bisque into a clean saucepan through a fine sieve lined with damp muslin, pressing down firmly on the solids to extract all the liquid. Add the cream and season with salt and cayenne pepper, then gently reheat. Garnish with the crab claws.

SERVES 4

ROUILLE

1 cooked russet potato, peeled and diced

1 red capsicum (pepper), grilled and peeled

2 garlic cloves, chopped

1 egg yolk

125 ml (4 fl oz/½ cup) olive oil

1 litre (35 fl oz/4 cups) fish stock

½ teaspoon saffron threads

4 thyme sprigs

5 cm (2 inch) piece orange peel

1 small baguette

olive oil, for brushing

300 g (10½ oz) salmon fillet, cut into 4 pieces

300 g (10½ oz) ling fillet, cut into 4 pieces

1 squid tube, cleaned and cut into rings

8 raw king prawns (shrimp), shelled and deveined

1   To make the rouille, place the potato, capsicum, garlic and egg yolk in a food processor and process until smooth. With the motor running, gradually add the olive oil until the mixture has the consistency of mayonnaise.

2   Preheat the oven to 180°C (350°F/Gas 4). Put the stock in a large saucepan and bring to the boil. Add the saffron, thyme and orange peel. Remove from the heat and leave to stand for 10 minutes to allow the flavours to infuse.

3   Meanwhile, cut the baguette into 1 cm (½ inch) slices. Brush with oil and put on a baking tray. Bake for 10 minutes, or until crisp and golden.

4   Strain the stock and return to the boil, then add the salmon, ling, squid rings and prawns. Remove the stock from the heat and leave for 2 minutes, or until the seafood is cooked. Serve with the rouille and croutons.

HEARTY SEAFOOD SOUP

SERVES 4

2 tablespoons dried shrimp

3 tablespoons olive oil

1 large onion, finely chopped

3 garlic cloves, crushed

1 small red chilli, deseeded and finely chopped

1 teaspoon finely grated fresh ginger

3 tablespoons crunchy peanut butter

800 g (1 lb 12 oz) tinned chopped tomatoes

50 g (1¾ oz) creamed coconut, chopped

400 ml (14 fl oz) coconut milk

pinch of ground cloves

4 tablespoons chopped coriander (cilantro) leaves

700 g (1 lb 9 oz) swordfish, cut into large chunks

100 g (3½ oz) small prawns (shrimp), peeled and deveined

2 tablespoons chopped cashew nuts

1 Soak the dried shrimp in boiling water for 10 minutes, then drain.

2 Heat the oil in a saucepan over medium heat. Cook the onion for 5 minutes. Add the garlic, chilli and ginger and cook for 2 minutes. Stir in the dried shrimp, peanut butter, tomato, creamed coconut, coconut milk, ground cloves and half of the coriander. Bring the mixture to the boil and simmer gently for 10 minutes. Remove from the heat, allow to cool slightly, then tip the sauce into a food processor or blender and blend until thick and smooth.

3 Return the sauce to the pan over medium heat. Add the swordfish and cook for 2 minutes, then add the prawns and continue to simmer until all the seafood is cooked—the prawns will be pink and the fish opaque. Serve with the cashews and remaining coriander sprinkled over the top.

CHUNKY FISH SOUP WITH BACON AND DUMPLINGS

SERVES 6

2 tablespoons olive oil

1 onion, chopped

1 small red capsicum (pepper), chopped

1 small zucchini (courgette), diced

150 g (5½ oz) smoked bacon, chopped

1 garlic clove, crushed

2 tablespoons paprika

400 g (14 oz) tinned chopped tomatoes

400 g (14 oz) tinned chickpeas

450 g (1 lb) skinless pike fillet, cut into large pieces

2 tablespoons chopped flat-leaf (Italian) parsley

DUMPLINGS

75 g (2½ oz) self-raising flour

1 egg, lightly beaten

1½ tablespoons milk

2 teaspoons finely chopped marjoram

1 Heat the oil in a saucepan over low heat. Add the onion and cook for 8 minutes, or until softened. Add the capsicum, zucchini, bacon and garlic and cook over medium heat for 5 minutes, stirring occasionally.

2 Meanwhile, to make the dumplings, combine the flour, egg, milk and marjoram in a bowl and mix with a wooden spoon.

3 Add the paprika, tomato, chickpeas and 800 ml (28 fl oz) water to the vegetables. Bring the liquid to the boil, then reduce the heat to low and simmer gently for 10 minutes, or until thickened slightly. Using two tablespoons to help you form the dumplings, add six rounds of the dumpling mixture to the soup. Poach for 2 minutes, then slide the pieces of fish into the liquid. Poach for a further 2–3 minutes, or until the fish is cooked. Season to taste and sprinkle with parsley

MANHATTAN-STYLE SEAFOOD CHOWDER

SERVES 4

60 g (2¼ oz) butter

3 bacon slices, chopped

2 onions, chopped

2 garlic cloves, finely chopped

2 celery stalks, sliced

3 potatoes, diced

3 teaspoons chopped thyme

1.25 litres (44 fl oz/5 cups) fish stock

1 kg (2 lb 4 oz) baby clams

1 tablespoon tomato paste
  (concentrated purée)

400 g (14 oz) tinned chopped tomatoes

375 g (13 oz) skinless ling fillets, cut into
  bite-sized pieces

12 large prawns (shrimp), peeled and
  deveined, tails intact

2 tablespoons chopped flat-leaf (Italian)
  parsley

1 **Melt the butter** in a saucepan over low heat. Add the bacon, onion, garlic and celery and cook, stirring occasionally, for 5 minutes, or until soft. Add the potato, thyme and 1 litre (35 fl oz/4 cups) of the stock to the saucepan and bring to the boil. Reduce the heat and simmer, covered, for 15 minutes. Pour the remaining stock into a saucepan and bring to the boil. Add the clams, cover and cook for 3–5 minutes, or until they open. Discard any that do not open. Drain the clam liquid through a muslin-lined sieve and add to the soup mixture. Pull most of the clams out of their shells, leaving a few intact to garnish.

2 **Stir the tomato paste** and chopped tomatoes into the soup and bring back to the boil. Add the fish, clams and prawns and simmer over low heat for 3 minutes, or until the seafood is cooked. Season and stir in the parsley. Serve garnished with the clams in their shells.

CARIBBEAN FISH SOUP

2 tomatoes

2 tablespoons oil

4 French shallots, finely chopped

2 celery stalks, chopped

1 large red capsicum (pepper), chopped

1 Scotch bonnet chilli, deseeded and finely chopped (see Note)

½ teaspoon ground allspice

½ teaspoon freshly grated nutmeg

850 ml (30 fl oz) fish stock

275 g (9¾ oz) orange sweet potato, peeled and cut into cubes

3 tablespoons lime juice

500 g (1 lb 2 oz) skinless sea bream fillets, cut into chunks

1 Score a cross in the base of each tomato. Soak in boiling water for 30 seconds, then plunge into cold water. Drain and peel the skin away from the cross. Chop the tomatoes, discarding the cores, and reserving any juices.

2 Heat the oil in a large saucepan, then add the shallots, celery, capsicum, chilli, allspice and nutmeg. Cook for 4–5 minutes, or until the vegetables have softened, stirring occasionally. Tip in the chopped tomatoes (including their juices) and stock and bring to the boil. Reduce the heat to medium and add the cubes of sweet potato. Season to taste and cook for about 15 minutes, or until the sweet potato is tender.

3 Add the lime juice and chunks of fish to the saucepan and poach gently for 4–5 minutes, or until the fish is cooked through. Season to taste.

Note: Scotch bonnet chillies looks like a mini capsicum (pepper) and can be green, red or orange. They are extremely hot but have a good, slightly acidic flavour.

JAPANESE PRAWN, SCALLOP AND NOODLE SOUP

SERVES 4

4 dried shiitake mushrooms

100 g (3½ oz) dried soba or
somen noodles

10 g (¼ oz) sachet bonito-flavoured
soup stock

75 g (2½ oz) carrot, cut into thin batons

150 g (5½ oz) firm tofu, cut into cubes

8 scallops, cleaned

16 prawns (shrimp), peeled and
deveined, tails intact

2 spring onions (scallions), finely
chopped

1 tablespoon mirin

shichimi togarashi, to serve (see Note)

1   Soak the mushrooms in 300 ml (10½ fl oz) of boiling water for 30 minutes. Cook the noodles in a saucepan of boiling water for 2 minutes, then drain and rinse with cold water. Return the noodles to the pan and cover.

2   In a saucepan, mix the stock with 1 litre (35 fl oz/4 cups) of water. Drain the mushrooms and add the soaking liquid to the pan. Chop the mushroom caps. Add the mushrooms and carrot to the pan and bring to the boil. Reduce the heat to a simmer and cook for 5 minutes. Add the tofu, scallops, prawns, spring onion and mirin. Simmer for 4 minutes, or until the prawns are pink.

3   Meanwhile, pour hot water over the noodles. Drain. Divide the noodles among four large bowls and pour the soup over, dividing the seafood equally. Serve sprinkled with shichimi togarashi.

Note: Shichimi togarashi is a Japanese condiment.

LOBSTER SOUP WITH ZUCCHINI AND AVOCADO

SERVES 4

50 g (1¾ oz) butter

1 garlic clove, crushed

2 French shallots, finely chopped

1 onion, chopped

1 zucchini (courgette), diced

2½ tablespoons dry white wine

400 ml (14 fl oz) fish stock

250 g (9 oz) raw lobster meat, chopped

250 ml (9 fl oz/1 cup) thick cream

1 avocado, diced

1 tablespoon chopped coriander
   (cilantro) leaves

1 tablespoon chopped flat-leaf (Italian)
   parsley

lemon juice, to serve

1 **Melt the butter** in a large saucepan over medium heat. Add the garlic, chopped shallots, onion and zucchini and cook for 8–10 minutes, or until the vegetables are just soft.

2 **Add the wine** and bring to the boil, then simmer for 3 minutes. Pour in the stock and bring to the boil again. Reduce the heat to low, add the lobster and simmer for 3–4 minutes, or until the lobster meat is opaque and tinged pink. Gently stir in the cream and season well.

3 **Ladle the soup** into four bowls and stir some of the avocado, coriander and parsley into each one. Squeeze a little lemon juice over the soup before serving.

CREAMY CLAM SOUP

SERVES 4

1.75 kg (4 lb) clams, cleaned

50 g (1¾ oz) butter

1 onion, chopped

1 celery stalk, chopped

1 large carrot, chopped

1 large leek, sliced into rings

250 g (9 oz) swede (rutabaga), diced

800 ml–1 litre (28–35 fl oz) fish stock

1 bay leaf

75 g (2½ oz/⅓ cup) medium or
    short-grain rice

200 ml (7 fl oz) cream

3 tablespoons finely chopped flat-leaf
    (Italian) parsley

1 Put the clams and 250 ml (9 fl oz/1 cup) water in a large saucepan. Bring to the boil, then reduce the heat to medium and cover with a tight-fitting lid. Cook for 3–4 minutes, or until the shells open. Strain into a bowl. Add enough stock to make up to 1 litre (35 fl oz/4 cups). Discard any clams that haven't opened. Remove all but eight of the clams from their shells.

2 Melt the butter in a saucepan. Add the vegetables and cook, covered, over medium heat for 10 minutes, stirring occasionally. Add the stock and bay leaf, bring to the boil, then reduce the heat and simmer for 10 minutes. Add the rice, bring back to the boil, cover and cook over medium heat for 15 minutes, or until the rice and vegetables are tender. Remove from the heat and stir in the clam meat. Remove the bay leaf and allow to cool for 10 minutes.

3 Purée the soup in a blender until smooth, then return to a saucepan. Stir in the cream and season. Gently reheat the soup. Add the parsley and two clams in the shell to each bowl.

NEW ENGLAND CLAM CHOWDER

SERVES 4

1.5 kg (3 lb 5 oz) clams, cleaned

2 teaspoons oil

3 bacon slices, chopped

1 onion, chopped

1 garlic clove, crushed

750 g (1 lb 10 oz) potatoes, diced

330 ml (11¼ fl oz/1⅓ cups) fish stock

500 ml (17 fl oz/2 cups) milk

125 ml (4 fl oz/½ cup) pouring cream

3 tablespoons chopped flat-leaf (Italian) parsley

1 Put the clams in a large heavy-based saucepan with 250 ml (9 fl oz/1 cup) of water. Cover and simmer for about 4 minutes, or until they open. Discard any that do not open. Strain the liquid through a muslin-lined sieve and reserve. Pull most of the clams out of their shells, leaving a few intact as a garnish.

2 Heat the oil in a saucepan. Add the bacon, onion and garlic and cook, stirring, over medium heat until the onion is soft and the bacon golden. Add the potato and stir well.

3 Add enough water to the reserved clam liquid to make 330 ml (11¼ fl oz/1⅓ cups) of liquid in total. Pour this and the stock into the saucepan and bring to the boil. Pour in the milk and bring back to the boil. Reduce the heat, cover and simmer for 20 minutes, or until the potato is tender. Uncover and simmer for 10 minutes, or until slightly thickened. Add the cream, clam meat and parsley and season. Heat through gently, but do not allow to boil. Serve with the clams in shells as a garnish.

CORN AND LEMONGRASS SOUP WITH YABBIES

SERVES 4

4 corn cobs

1 tablespoon oil

1 leek, white part only, chopped

1 celery stick, chopped

3 lemongrass stems, white part only, bruised

5 garlic cloves, crushed

1 teaspoon ground cumin

1 teaspoon ground coriander

¾ teaspoon ground white pepper

3 kaffir lime leaves

750 ml (26 fl oz/3 cups) chicken stock

800 ml (28 fl oz) coconut milk

125 ml (4 fl oz/½ cup) cream

2 teaspoons butter

½ teaspoon sambal oelek

1.2 kg (2 lb 12 oz) cooked yabbies or crayfish, shredded

1 tablespoon finely chopped coriander (cilantro) leaves

1 Trim the kernels from the corn. Heat the oil in a saucepan over medium heat. Add the leek, celery and lemon grass. Stir for 10 minutes, or until the leek is soft. Add half the garlic, and the cumin, coriander and ½ teaspoon of the pepper. Cook, stirring, for 1–2 minutes, or until fragrant. Add the corn, lime leaves, stock and coconut milk, stir well and simmer, for 1½ hours. Remove from the heat and cool. Remove the lemon grass and lime leaves and blend the mixture in batches in a food processor.

2 Push the mixture through a sieve. Repeat. Return to a saucepan, add the cream and warm gently.

3 Melt the butter in a frying pan over medium heat, add the remaining garlic, sambal oelek, remaining pepper and a pinch of salt and stir for 1 minute. Add the yabby meat, stir for a further minute, then remove from the heat and stir in the coriander.

PRAWN, POTATO AND CORN CHOWDER

SERVES 4–6

600 g (1 lb 5 oz) raw prawns (shrimp)

3 corn cobs, husks removed

1 tablespoon olive oil

2 leeks, white part only, finely chopped

2 garlic cloves, crushed

650 g (1 lb 7 oz) potatoes, cut into
  1.5 cm (5/8 inch) cubes

750 ml (26 fl oz/3 cups) fish stock

375 ml (13 fl oz/1½ cups) milk

250 ml (9 fl oz/1 cup) cream

pinch of cayenne pepper

3 tablespoons finely chopped flat-leaf
  (Italian) parsley

1 **Peel and devein** the prawns, then chop into 1.5 cm (5/8 inch) pieces. Cut the kernels from the corn cobs.

2 **Heat the oil** in a large saucepan and add the leek. Cook over medium–low heat for about 5 minutes, or until soft and lightly golden. Add the garlic and cook for 30 seconds, then add the corn, potato, stock and milk.

3 **Bring to the boil,** then reduce the heat. Simmer, partially covered, for 20 minutes, or until the potato is soft but still holds its shape. Remove the lid and simmer for a further 10 minutes to allow the soup to thicken. Reduce the heat to low.

4 **Put 500 ml** (17 fl oz/2 cups) of the soup in a blender and blend until very smooth.

5 **Return the blended soup** to the saucepan and add the prawns. Increase the heat to medium and simmer for 2 minutes, or until the prawns are pink and cooked through. Stir in the cream, cayenne pepper and 2 tablespoons of the parsley. Season to taste, then serve garnished with the remaining parsley.

TOM YUM GOONG

SERVES 4–6

1 tablespoon oil

500 g (1 lb 2 oz) prawns (shrimp), peeled and deveined, reserving the heads and shells

2 tablespoons Thai red curry paste or tom yum paste

2 tablespoons tamarind purée (see Note)

2 teaspoons ground turmeric

1 teaspoon chopped red chillies

4 kaffir lime leaves, shredded

2 tablespoons fish sauce

2 tablespoons lime juice

2 teaspoons grated palm sugar or soft brown sugar

2 tablespoons coriander (cilantro) leaves

1 Heat the oil in a large saucepan or wok and cook the prawn heads and shells for 10 minutes over medium heat, stirring frequently, until the heads are deep orange in colour.

2 Add 250 ml (9 fl oz/1 cup) of water and the curry paste to the saucepan. Bring to the boil and cook for 5 minutes, or until reduced slightly. Add another 2 litres (70 fl oz/8 cups) of water and simmer for 20 minutes. Strain, discarding the shells and heads, and pour the stock back into the pan.

3 Add the tamarind, turmeric, chillies and lime leaves to the saucepan. Bring to the boil and cook for 2 minutes. Add the prawns and cook for 5 minutes, or until pink. Stir in the fish sauce, lime juice and sugar. Serve sprinkled with coriander leaves.

Note: If you are unable to find tamarind purée, you can make your own by soaking a 225 g (8 oz) packet of tamarind pulp in 500 ml (17 fl oz/2 cups) of boiling water for 1–2 hours, crushing occasionally. Push through a sieve and discard the fibres. Alternatively, use lemon juice.

ROUX

4 tablespoons oil

75 g (2½ oz/⅔ cup) plain (all-purpose) flour

1 onion, finely chopped

4 crabs, cleaned

450 g (1 lb) chorizo sausage

6 spring onions (scallions), sliced

1 green capsicum (pepper), roughly chopped

3 tablespoons chopped flat-leaf (Italian) parsley

¼ teaspoon chilli powder

500 g (1 lb 2 oz) prawns (shrimp), peeled and deveined

24 oysters, shucked

½ teaspoon filé powder (see Note)

1½ tablespoons long-grain rice

1 To make the roux, pour the oil into a heavy-based saucepan over low heat. Add the flour, stirring after each addition, to make a thin roux. Continue to stir over low heat for 35 minutes, or until dark brown. Add the onion and cook for 4 minutes, or until tender. Pour in 1.5 litres (52 fl oz/6 cups) of boiling water, stirring to dissolve the roux, and bring to a simmer.

2 Cut the crabs into pieces. Cut the chorizo into pieces. Add the crab, sausage, spring onion, capsicum, parsley and chilli powder to the roux. Cook for about 30 minutes, then add the prawns and the oysters and their juices and cook for a further 5 minutes, or until the prawns are pink. Season, then stir in the filé powder.

3 Meanwhile, cook the rice in salted boiling water for about 10 minutes, or until just cooked through. Put a couple of tablespoons of rice in the bottom of each bowl and ladle over the gumbo. Serve immediately.

Note: Filé powder is a flavouring often used in Creole cooking. It is made by drying, then grinding sassafras leaves.

HOT AND SOUR PRAWN SOUP

SERVES 4–6

350 g (12 oz) raw prawns (shrimp)

1 tablespoon oil

3 lemongrass stems, white part only

3 thin slices fresh galangal

3–5 small fresh red chillies

5 kaffir lime leaves, finely shredded

2 tablespoons fish sauce

2 spring onions (scallions), sliced

70 g (2½ oz/½ cup) tinned straw mushrooms, drained, or quartered button mushrooms

3 tablespoons lime juice

1–2 tablespoons chilli paste, or to taste

coriander (cilantro) leaves, to garnish (optional)

1 Peel and devein the prawns, leaving the tail intact and reserving the heads and shells.

2 Heat the oil in a large stockpot or wok and add the prawn heads and shells. Cook for 5 minutes, or until the shells turn bright orange. Bruise 1 stem of the lemon grass with the back of a knife. Add to the pan with the galangal and 2 litres (70 fl oz/8 cups) water. Bring to the boil, then reduce the heat and simmer for 20 minutes. Strain the stock and return to the pan. Discard the shells and herbs.

3 Finely slice the chillies and remaining lemon grass. Add to the liquid with the lime leaves, fish sauce, spring onion and mushrooms. Cook gently for 2 minutes.

4 Add the prawns and cook for 3 minutes, or until the prawns are tender. Add the lime juice and chilli paste (adjust to taste with extra lime juice or fish sauce). If desired, garnish with coriander leaves.

MEXICAN SOUP WITH SALSA

SERVES 4

3 tablespoons olive oil

1 large onion, chopped

1 large celery stalk, chopped

3 garlic cloves, crushed

2 thin red chillies, chopped

200 ml (7 fl oz) fish stock

800 g (1 lb 12 oz) tinned chopped
   tomatoes

2 bay leaves

1 teaspoon dried oregano

1 teaspoon caster (superfine) sugar

2 corn cobs, kernels removed

500 g (1 lb 2 oz) halibut fillets

2 tablespoons chopped coriander
   (cilantro) leaves

juice of 2 limes

12 prawns (shrimp), tails intact

8 scallops, cleaned

12 clams, cleaned

125 g (4½ oz/½ cup) cream

SALSA

½ small avocado

1 tablespoon coriander (cilantro) leaves

grated zest and juice of 1 lime

½ red onion, finely chopped

1   Heat the oil in a saucepan. Add the onion and celery and cook over medium heat for 10 minutes. Add the garlic and chilli and cook for 1 minute, stirring. Add the fish stock and tomatoes. Stir in the bay leaves, oregano and sugar and bring to the boil. Reduce the heat to low and simmer for 10 minutes. Remove the bay leaves, then tip the tomato mixture into a food processor and whiz until smooth. Return the tomato sauce to the pan and season. Add the corn kernels and bring back to the boil. Reduce the heat and simmer for 3 minutes. Cut the fish into chunks. Stir the coriander and the lime juice into the sauce, add the fish to the pan, then simmer for 1 minute. Add the prawns, scallops and clams. Cover with a lid and cook for a further 2–3 minutes, or until the seafood is cooked through.

2   To make the salsa, chop the avocado into cubes and mix with the coriander, the lime zest and juice, and red onion. Stir the cream into the soup and top with salsa.

BOUILLABAISSE

SERVES 6

ROUILLE
1 small red capsicum (pepper)

1 slice of white bread

1 red chilli

2 garlic cloves

1 egg yolk

4 tablespoons olive oil

SOUP
2 tablespoons oil

1 fennel bulb, thinly sliced

1 onion, chopped

750 g (1 lb 10 oz) ripe tomatoes

1.25 litres (44 fl oz/5 cups) fish stock

pinch of saffron threads

bouquet garni

5 cm (2 inch) piece orange zest

1.5 kg (3 lb 5 oz) monkfish fillets, cut
into pieces

18 black mussels, cleaned

1 **To make the rouille,** cut the capsicum in half, remove the seeds and membrane and place, skin-side up, under the grill (broiler) until the skin blackens. Cool, then peel away the skin. Chop the capsicum flesh. Soak the bread in 3 tablespoons of water, then squeeze dry. Put the capsicum, bread, chilli, garlic and egg yolk in a food processor and process. Add the oil, mixing until smooth. Cover and refrigerate.

2 **Heat the oil** in a large saucepan. Cook the fennel and onion for 5 minutes.

3 **Score a cross** in the base of each tomato. Cover with boiling water for 30 seconds, then plunge into cold water. Drain and peel the skin. Chop the tomatoes.

4 **Add the tomato** to the saucepan and cook for 3 minutes. Stir in the stock, saffron, bouquet garni and orange zest, bring to the boil and boil for 10 minutes. Remove the bouquet garni and orange zest and purée in a blender. Return to the saucepan, season and bring back to the boil. Reduce the heat to a simmer and add the fish and mussels. Cook for 5 minutes, or until the fish is tender and the mussels have opened. Discard any mussels that haven't opened. Serve the soup with rouille.

MEDITERRANEAN FISH SOUP

SERVES 4

1 kg (2 lb 4 oz) white fish fillets

3 tablespoons olive oil

2 large onions, chopped

1–2 garlic cloves, crushed

4 large tomatoes, peeled, seeded and chopped

2 tablespoons tomato paste (purée)

6 tablespoons chopped gherkins

1 tablespoon chopped capers

1 tablespoon pitted and chopped green olives

1 tablespoon pitted and chopped black olives

750 ml (26 fl oz/3 cups) fish stock

250 ml (9 fl oz/1 cup) white wine

1 bay leaf

15 g (¼ oz) chopped basil

60 g (2¼ oz) chopped parsley

1 **Remove the skin** and bones from the fish and chop into bite-sized pieces. Heat the oil in a large heavy-based pan and cook the onion and garlic for 8 minutes until soft.

2 **Stir in the tomato** and paste. Stir for 2–3 minutes, or until the tomato is soft. Stir in the gherkins and half the capers and olives.

3 **Add the fish,** stock, wine and bay leaf and season. Bring slowly to the boil, reduce the heat and simmer for 10–12 minutes, or until the fish is just cooked. Stir in the herbs. Add the remaining capers and olives. Serve.

VEGETABLE

WATERCRESS, LEEK AND POTATO SOUP

SERVES 4

350 g (12 oz) watercress, trimmed

1 tablespoon oil

1 leek, white part only, chopped

2 garlic cloves, chopped

1 celery stalk, chopped

1 teaspoon freshly grated nutmeg

500 g (1 lb 2 oz) potatoes, chopped

1 litre (35 fl oz/4 cups) vegetable stock
   or chicken stock

250 ml (9 fl oz/1 cup) milk

1 handful mint

1 **Reserve a few watercress** leaves for serving. Pick off the remaining leaves in bunches, discarding the thick stems. Roughly chop and reserve the watercress.

2 **Heat the oil** in a large heavy-based saucepan. Add the leek, garlic and celery. Stir for 2 minutes to coat the vegetables in the oil. Reduce the heat, cover and simmer, stirring occasionally, for 5 minutes. Do not allow the vegetables to brown.

3 **Add the nutmeg,** potato and stock. Slowly bring to the boil, then reduce the heat and simmer, covered, for 20 minutes. Stir in the chopped watercress. Set aside to cool for 10 minutes.

4 **Stir the milk** and mint into the soup. Using an immersion blender fitted with the chopping blade, whizz for 1 minute, or until puréed to the desired consistency.

5 **Gently reheat the soup** and season well with salt and freshly ground black pepper. Ladle into bowls and garnish with the reserved watercress leaves.

CREAMY BRUSSELS SPROUT AND LEEK SOUP

SERVES 4

1 tablespoon olive oil

2 rindless bacon slices, chopped

2 garlic cloves, chopped

3 leeks, white part only, sliced

300 g (10½ oz) brussels sprouts, roughly chopped

750 ml (26 fl oz/3 cups) vegetable stock or chicken stock

185 ml (6 fl oz/¾ cup) cream or milk

slices of toasted crusty bread, to serve

1 **Heat the oil** in a large saucepan over medium heat. Add the chopped bacon and fry for 3 minutes. Add the garlic and leek, cover and fry, stirring often, for a further 5 minutes. Add the brussels sprouts, stir to combine, cover and cook, stirring often, for 5 minutes.

2 **Add the stock** and season with salt and freshly ground black pepper. Bring to the boil, then reduce the heat, cover the pan and simmer for 10 minutes, or until the vegetables are very tender. Set aside to cool for 10 minutes.

3 **Using an immersion blender** fitted with the chopping blade, whizz the soup for 25–30 seconds, or until puréed. Stir through the cream or milk and gently reheat the soup. Serve with slices of toasted crusty bread.

Note: For a vegetarian version of this soup, simply omit the bacon and use vegetable stock rather than chicken stock.

BEETROOT AND RED CAPSICUM SOUP

SERVES 4

6 beetroot (beets), without stems and leaves

1 tablespoon oil

1 red onion, chopped

1 celery stalk, chopped

1 garlic clove, chopped

1 large red capsicum (pepper), seeded and chopped

410 g (14½ oz) tinned chopped tomatoes

1 tablespoon red wine vinegar

sour cream, to serve

2 tablespoons finely snipped chives, to serve

1 Wearing protective gloves, peel the beetroot with a vegetable peeler and cut it into 3 cm (1¼ inch) dice. Put the beetroot in a large saucepan with 1 litre (35 fl oz/4 cups) of water. Slowly bring to the boil over medium–low heat, then reduce the heat and simmer for 25–30 minutes, or until the beetroot is tender when pierced with a fork. Remove about ½ cup of beetroot cubes, dice finely and set aside.

2 Meanwhile, heat the oil in a large heavy-based saucepan over medium heat. Add the onion, celery, garlic and capsicum and stir to coat the vegetables in the oil. Reduce the heat to low, cover and cook, stirring occasionally, for 10 minutes. Do not allow the vegetables to brown. Add the chopped tomatoes and vinegar and simmer for 10 minutes.

3 Transfer the tomato mixture to the saucepan containing the beetroot and remove the pan from the heat. Using an immersion blender fitted with the chopping blade, whizz the soup for 20–30 seconds, or until smooth. Season well with salt and freshly ground black pepper.

4 Ladle the soup into four warm bowls and top with a spoonful of sour cream, the reserved diced beetroot and the chives.

Note: The soup will keep in the refrigerator, covered, for up to 4 days, or in an airtight container in the freezer for up to 1 month.

ALSACE MUSHROOM SOUP

SERVES 4

10 g (¼ oz) dried porcini mushrooms

250 ml (9 fl oz/1 cup) hot water

50 g (1¾ oz) butter

1 onion, roughly chopped

4 French shallots, chopped

1 large potato (about 185 g/6½ oz), chopped

1 celery stalk, chopped

2 garlic cloves, chopped

1 small red chilli, seeded and chopped

175 g (6 oz) flat mushrooms, roughly chopped

175 g (6 oz) Swiss brown mushrooms, roughly chopped

750 ml (26 fl oz/3 cups) chicken stock or vegetable stock

2 large thyme sprigs

1–2 teaspoons lemon juice, to taste

90 g (3¼ oz/⅓ cup) sour cream, to serve

2 tablespoons finely chopped flat-leaf (Italian) parsley, to serve

1 tablespoon grated lemon zest, to serve

1 **Put the porcini mushrooms** in a small bowl and pour over the hot water. Set aside to soften for 10 minutes.

2 **Meanwhile,** heat the butter in a large heavy-based saucepan. Add the onion, shallots, potato, celery, garlic and chilli. Stir for 2 minutes to coat the vegetables in the butter. Reduce the heat, cover and simmer, stirring occasionally, for 5 minutes. Do not allow the vegetables to brown.

3 **Add** the fresh mushrooms to the saucepan and cook, stirring, for 2–3 minutes. Add the stock, thyme sprigs and porcini mushrooms with their soaking water. Slowly bring to the boil over low heat, then reduce the heat and simmer, covered, for 15 minutes. Discard the thyme sprigs. Set aside to cool slightly.

4 **Using an immersion blender** fitted with the chopping blade, whizz the soup for 15–20 seconds, or until roughly puréed. The soup should still have texture. Add the lemon juice, to taste, and season well with salt and freshly ground black pepper.

5 **Gently reheat** the soup and ladle into warm bowls. Top with a spoonful of the sour cream and sprinkle with the parsley and lemon zest.

SPICED PUMPKIN AND LENTIL SOUP

SERVES 4

1 kg (2 lb 4 oz) pumpkin (squash)

2 tablespoons olive oil

1 large onion, chopped

3 garlic cloves, chopped

1 teaspoon ground turmeric

½ teaspoon ground coriander

½ teaspoon ground cumin

½ teaspoon chilli flakes

135 g (4¾ oz/½ cup) red lentils, rinsed
   and drained

1 litre (35 fl oz/4 cups) boiling water

90 g (3¼ oz/⅓ cup) plain yoghurt,
   to serve

1 Peel, seed and cube the pumpkin to give 700 g
(1 lb 9 oz/4½ cups) of flesh.

2 Heat the oil in a large saucepan over medium heat.
Add the onion and garlic and fry for 5 minutes, or until
softened, being careful not to burn the garlic. Add the
turmeric, coriander, cumin and chilli flakes and fry, stirring
constantly, for 2 minutes.

3 Add the pumpkin, red lentils and boiling water. Bring to
the boil, then reduce the heat and simmer, covered, for
20 minutes, or until the pumpkin and lentils are tender. Set
aside to cool for 5 minutes.

4 Using an immersion blender fitted with the chopping
blade, whizz the soup for 25–35 seconds, or until evenly
chopped. Season well with salt and freshly ground black
pepper and reheat the soup.

5 Ladle the soup into four bowls, top with a spoonful of the
yoghurt and sprinkle with freshly ground black pepper.

ROASTED LEEK AND CELERIAC SOUP

SERVES 4

2 tablespoons olive oil

800 g (1 lb 12 oz/about 2 large) leeks, white part only, cut into 5 cm (2 inch) lengths

1 garlic bulb, unpeeled, halved

800 g (1 lb 12 oz) celeriac, chopped

250 ml (9 fl oz/1 cup) milk

125 ml (4 fl oz/½ cup) thick cream

2 tablespoons snipped chives

slices of toasted baguette, to serve

1 **Preheat the oven** to 200°C (400°F/Gas 6). Put the olive oil in a roasting tin and heat in the oven for 5 minutes. Add the leek and garlic bulb halves and season with salt and freshly ground black pepper. Shake the roasting tin to coat the vegetables with the oil. Roast for 20–25 minutes, or until the leek is tender. Remove the leek and roast the garlic for a further 10–15 minutes, or until tender when pierced with the tip of a knife.

2 **Meanwhile,** put the celeriac and 750 ml (26 fl oz/3 cups) of water in a large saucepan. Cover and bring to the boil, then reduce the heat to medium–low and simmer for 20 minutes, or until tender. Add the roasted leek.

3 **Squeeze or scoop** the garlic into the saucepan. Season with salt and freshly ground black pepper and mix well. Add the milk.

4 **Remove the saucepan** from the heat. Using an immersion blender fitted with the chopping blade, whizz for 45 seconds, or until puréed. Stir through the cream and gently reheat the soup. Check the seasoning and thickness, adding additional milk if the soup is too thick. Sprinkle with the chives and serve topped with slices of toasted baguette.

SPICY CORN AND COCONUT SOUP

SERVES 4

1 tablespoon oil

1 large onion, chopped

1 celery stalk, chopped

2 garlic cloves, chopped

1 teaspoon ground coriander

1½ teaspoons ground cumin

1–2 teaspoons sambal oelek (see Note)

500 g (1 lb 2 oz) potatoes, chopped

750 ml (26 fl oz/3 cups) chicken stock or vegetable stock

420 g (14¾ oz) tinned corn kernels, drained

270 ml (9½ fl oz) light coconut milk

1 handful coriander (cilantro) leaves

310 g (11 oz) tinned creamed corn

extra coriander (cilantro) leaves, to serve

1 Heat the oil in a large heavy-based saucepan over medium–low heat. Add the onion, celery and garlic. Stir for 2 minutes to coat the vegetables in the oil. Reduce the heat, cover and simmer, stirring occasionally, for 5 minutes. Do not allow the vegetables to brown.

2 Add the ground coriander, cumin and 1 teaspoon of the sambal oelek and stir for 1 minute. Add the potato and stock. Bring slowly to the boil, then reduce the heat and simmer, covered, for 15 minutes, or until the potato is cooked. Stir in the corn kernels, coconut milk and coriander leaves. Set aside to cool slightly.

3 Using an immersion blender fitted with the chopping blade, whizz the soup for 20–30 seconds, or until smooth. Stir in the creamed corn and gently reheat the soup. Add a little hot water if you prefer a thinner consistency. Season well. Ladle into four warm bowls and add the remaining sambal oelek, to taste. Sprinkle with the extra coriander leaves.

Note: Sambal oelek is a fiery condiment used in Malaysian, Indonesian and Singaporean cuisines. It is made from red chillies, vinegar and sugar and is available in jars from Asian supermarkets.

CHILLED CUCUMBER YOGHURT SOUP

SERVES 4

2 telegraph (long) cucumbers, about 550 g (1 lb 4 oz)

1 large handful mint

2 garlic cloves, chopped

1 teaspoon dried mint

125 ml (4 fl oz/½ cup) milk

500 g (1 lb 2 oz/2 cups) Greek-style yoghurt

2–3 teaspoons lemon juice, to taste

3–4 drops Tabasco sauce, to taste

2 tablespoons finely snipped chives, to serve

1 Peel the cucumbers, halve them lengthways and scoop out the seeds. Set aside about one-third of one of the cucumbers.

2 Put the remaining cucumber in a small processor fitted with the metal blade. Add the mint, garlic, dried mint and milk and whizz in 3–4 second bursts for 20 seconds. Add the yoghurt, and the lemon juice and Tabasco sauce to taste, and season well with salt and freshly ground black pepper. Whizz until well combined and smooth.

3 Transfer the soup to a bowl, cover and refrigerate for at least 2 hours to allow the flavours to develop.

4 Finely dice the reserved cucumber. Ladle the soup into bowls and top with the diced cucumber and chives.

Note: The soup should be consumed within 1 day. It is not suitable for freezing.

SWEET POTATO, CHILLI AND CORIANDER SOUP

SERVES 4

6 whole coriander (cilantro) plants
(roots, stems and leaves)

1 small red chilli, seeded and roughly
chopped

2 garlic cloves, chopped

1 tablespoon oil

1 large onion, chopped

1 celery stalk, chopped

650 g (1 lb 7 oz) orange sweet potato,
cut into 5 cm (2 inch) pieces

1 litre (35 fl oz/4 cups) vegetable stock
or chicken stock

145 ml (4¾ fl oz) coconut milk

1 Remove the leaves from the coriander plants. Reserve a few whole leaves for garnishing and chop the remainder of the leaves. Set aside. Thoroughly wash the roots and stems and chop roughly. Put in a mini processor and add the chilli and garlic. Add 2 teaspoons of the oil and whizz for 20 seconds, or until the mixture forms a rough paste.

2 Heat the remaining oil in a large heavy-based saucepan. Add the paste and stir over low heat for 2 minutes, or until aromatic. Stir in the onion and celery. Cover and cook for 5 minutes, stirring once or twice. Do not allow the mixture to brown.

3 Add the sweet potato and stir to coat in the mixture. Cook for 2 minutes, then add the stock. Bring to the boil, then reduce the heat, cover and cook for 20 minutes, or until the sweet potato is tender. Set aside to cool slightly.

4 Using an immersion blender fitted with the chopping blade, whizz the soup until smooth. Season well with salt and freshly ground black pepper. Stir in the coconut milk and gently reheat the soup. Add the chopped coriander leaves and serve garnished with the reserved whole coriander leaves.

Note: The soup can also be served chilled. It will keep in the refrigerator, covered, for up to 5 days, or in an airtight container in the freezer for up to 1 month.

BROAD BEAN SOUP WITH MIXED HERB PASTE

SERVES 4

1 kg (2 lb 4 oz) broad (fava) beans, shelled

2 tablespoons olive oil

2 large leeks, white part only, sliced

1 large onion, chopped

2 celery stalks, sliced

3 garlic cloves, finely chopped

50 g (1¾ oz) sliced pancetta, cut into matchsticks

1 teaspoon ground cumin

1.25 litres (44 fl oz/5 cups) vegetable stock or chicken stock

snipped chives, to serve

HERB PASTE

1 small handful mint

1 small handful basil

1 small handful flat-leaf (Italian) parsley

½ teaspoon grated lemon zest

1 garlic clove, chopped

2 tablespoons toasted pine nuts

4 tablespoons olive oil

1 Soak the broad beans in boiling water for 3–4 minutes, then drain. When cool enough to handle, slip off the skins.

2 Gently heat the oil in a heavy-based frying pan over medium heat. Add the leek, onion and celery and sauté for 6 minutes, or until the vegetables are softened but not browned. Increase the heat to medium–high, add the garlic, pancetta and cumin and fry, stirring constantly, for 1 minute.

3 Transfer the pancetta mixture to a large saucepan and add the broad beans and stock. Bring to the boil over medium heat, then reduce the heat and simmer for 10 minutes.

4 Remove the saucepan from the heat. Using an immersion blender fitted with the chopping blade, whizz the soup for 1 minute, or until smooth. Season with salt and freshly ground black pepper, to taste.

5 To make the herb paste, put the mint, basil, parsley, lemon zest, garlic and pine nuts in a small processor fitted with the metal blade. Whizz until roughly chopped. With the motor running, gradually add the olive oil and continue whizzing for 45–60 seconds, or until the mixture has a paste-like consistency.

6 Divide the soup among four bowls and top with the herb paste and chives.

SPINACH AND LENTIL SOUP

SERVES 4

250 g (9 oz/1⅓ cups) green lentils, rinsed and picked over

1.5 litres (52 fl oz/6 cups) chicken stock

3 tablespoons olive oil

1 large onion, finely chopped

1 fennel bulb, trimmed and finely diced

1 large carrot, finely diced

½ teaspoon fennel seeds

¼ teaspoon cayenne pepper

2 bay leaves

90 g (3¼ oz/⅓ cup) tomato paste (concentrated purée)

3 garlic cloves, halved lengthways and thinly sliced

3 large handfuls baby English spinach

small pinch of sweet smoked paprika

extra virgin olive oil, to serve

1 **Put the lentils** in a large saucepan and cover with cold water. Bring to the boil over medium–high heat, then reduce the heat and simmer for 10 minutes. Drain and return to the saucepan. Add the stock and 500 ml (17 fl oz/2 cups) of water and bring to the boil. Reduce the heat to medium and simmer for 15 minutes.

2 **Meanwhile,** gently heat 2 tablespoons of the oil in a heavy-based frying pan. Add the onion, fennel, carrot, fennel seeds and cayenne pepper. Lightly crush the bay leaves in your hand and add them to the pan. Sauté over low heat for 5 minutes, or until the onion is translucent but not browned. Stir through the tomato paste. Add the onion mixture to the lentils and simmer, partially covered, for 20 minutes, or until the lentils and vegetables are tender.

3 **Gently heat** the remaining oil in a frying pan over low heat. Add the garlic and 2 handfuls of the spinach and cook, stirring, for 2–3 minutes, or until the spinach has wilted. Add the paprika. Add the spinach mixture to the soup and simmer for 2 minutes.

4 **Remove the saucepan** from the heat and discard the bay leaves. Transfer half the soup to a blender or small processor fitted with the metal blade. Whizz for 30 seconds, or until smooth. Return the puréed soup to the saucepan and add the remaining spinach. Season to taste. Drizzle with extra virgin olive oil and sprinkle with freshly ground black pepper

ROASTED TOMATO, ALMOND AND BASIL SOUP

SERVES 4

3 tablespoons olive oil

1 kg (2 lb 4 oz) large, vine-ripened
   tomatoes

1 large onion, finely chopped

2 garlic cloves, thinly sliced

50 g (1¾ oz/⅓ cup) blanched almonds,
   roughly chopped

2 handfuls basil, roughly torn

750 ml (26 fl oz/3 cups) chicken stock

1 **Preheat the oven** to 180°C (350°F/Gas 4). Grease a baking tray with 1 tablespoon of the oil. Cut the tomatoes in half, scoop out the seeds and arrange, cut side down, on the prepared tray. Roast for 15 minutes, then remove from the oven and set aside until the tomatoes are cool enough to handle. Discard the tomato skin and roughly chop the flesh.

2 **Heat the remaining oil** in a large saucepan over medium–low heat. Gently sauté the onion and garlic for 5–6 minutes, or until soft and translucent. Add the chopped tomato, almonds and half the basil. Fry, stirring once or twice, for 5 minutes.

3 **Transfer the mixture** to a small processor fitted with the metal blade and whizz for 15–20 seconds, or until thick and smooth.

4 **Return the mixture** to the saucepan, stir in the stock and bring to the boil over medium–high heat. Stir in the remaining basil, season with salt and freshly ground black pepper, to taste, and serve immediately.

PUMPKIN AND CARROT SOUP

SERVES 4–6

40 g (1½ oz) butter

1 large onion, chopped

2 garlic cloves, crushed

500 g (1 lb 2 oz) carrots, sliced

125 ml (4 fl oz/½ cup) orange juice

750 g (1 lb 10 oz) butternut pumpkin
(squash), peeled and roughly chopped

1.5 litres (52 fl oz/6 cups) chicken stock

1 tablespoon snipped chives

herb scones or herb bread, to serve

1   Melt the butter in a large saucepan over medium heat and cook the onion for 5 minutes, or until soft and starting to brown. Add the garlic and carrot and cook for another 5 minutes, or until starting to soften. Pour in the orange juice and bring to the boil over high heat. Add the pumpkin, stock and 500 ml (17 fl oz/2 cups) water and return to the boil. Reduce the heat and simmer for 30 minutes, or until the carrot and pumpkin are soft.

2   Blend the soup in batches in a blender until smooth—add a little more stock if you prefer the soup to be a thinner consistency.

3   Return to the cleaned pan and reheat. Season to taste with salt and freshly ground pepper. Divide the soup among serving bowls and garnish with the chives. Serve with herb scones or bread.

LEEK AND POTATO SOUP

SERVES 6

50 g (1¾ oz) butter

1 onion, finely chopped

3 leeks, white part only, sliced

1 celery stalk, finely chopped

1 garlic clove, finely chopped

200 g (7 oz) potatoes, chopped

750 ml (26 fl oz/3 cups) chicken stock

220 ml (7½ fl oz) cream

2 tablespoons chopped chives

1 Melt the butter in a large saucepan and add the onion, leek, celery and garlic. Cover the pan and cook, stirring occasionally, over low heat for 15 minutes, or until the vegetables are softened but not browned. Add the potato and stock and bring to the boil.

2 Reduce the heat and leave to simmer, covered, for 20 minutes. Allow the soup to cool a little before puréeing in a blender or food processor. Return to the cleaned saucepan.

3 Bring the soup gently back to the boil and stir in the cream. Season with salt and white pepper and reheat without boiling. Serve hot or well chilled, garnished with chives.

TOMATO AND BREAD SOUP

SERVES 4

750 g (1 lb 10 oz) vine-ripened tomatoes

1 loaf (450 g/1 lb) day-old crusty
   Italian bread

1 tablespoon olive oil

3 garlic cloves, crushed

1 tablespoon tomato paste
   (concentrated purée)

1.25 litres (44 fl oz/5 cups) hot vegetable
   stock

4 tablespoons torn basil leaves

2–3 tablespoons extra virgin olive oil,
   plus extra, to serve

1 Score a cross in the base of each tomato. Place in a bowl of boiling water for 1 minute, then plunge into cold water and peel the skin away from the cross. Cut the tomatoes in half and scoop out the seeds with a teaspoon. Chop the tomato flesh.

2 Remove most of the crust from the bread and discard. Cut the bread into 3 cm (1¼ inch) pieces.

3 Heat the oil in a large saucepan. Add the garlic, tomato and tomato paste, then reduce the heat and simmer, stirring occasionally, for 15 minutes until thickened. Add the stock and bring to the boil, stirring for 2 minutes. Reduce the heat to medium, add the bread pieces and cook, stirring, for 5 minutes, or until the bread softens and absorbs most of the liquid. Add more stock or water if necessary.

4 Stir in the torn basil leaves and extra virgin olive oil, and leave for 5 minutes so the flavours have time to develop. Drizzle with a little of the extra oil.

Note: This soup is popular in Italy in the summer months when tomatoes are at their tastiest, and as a way of using up leftover bread. In Italy, the soup is called Pappa al pomodoro.

ASPARAGUS SOUP WITH PARMESAN CRISPS

SERVES 4

725 g (1 lb 9½ oz) fresh asparagus, trimmed

1 tablespoon vegetable oil

30 g (1 oz) butter

1 large red onion, finely chopped

1 large leek, thinly sliced

2 large potatoes, cut into 1 cm (½ inch) cubes

1.25 litres (44 fl oz/5 cups) chicken stock

4 tablespoons cream

90 g (3¼ oz/⅓ cup) sour cream

1 tablespoon snipped chives

60 g (2¼ oz/⅔ cup) grated parmesan cheese

1 **Roughly chop** 650 g (1 lb 7 oz) of the asparagus and cut the rest into 6 cm (2½ inch) pieces. Heat the oil and butter in a large saucepan over medium heat and cook the onion and leek for 5 minutes, or until soft. Add the potato, chopped asparagus and chicken stock and bring to the boil over high heat. Reduce the heat and simmer for 8 minutes, or until the vegetables are tender. Blanch the remaining asparagus in a saucepan of boiling water.

2 **To make the parmesan crisps,** preheat the oven to 190°C (375°F/Gas 5). Line three baking trays with baking paper and place four 9 cm (3½ inch) egg rings on each tray. Sprinkle 5 g (⅛ oz) of the parmesan into each ring in a thin layer. For a lacy edge, remove the rings. Bake for 5 minutes, or until melted and just golden brown. Allow to cool.

3 **Cool the soup,** then purée it. Return to the pan and stir in the cream for 1–2 minutes, or until heated through. Season. Garnish with sour cream, the blanched asparagus and chives. Serve with the parmesan crisps.

LENTIL AND VEGETABLE SOUP WITH SPICED YOGHURT

SERVES 4

1 zucchini (courgette)

1 head of broccoli, trimmed

150 g (5½ oz) green beans, trimmed

155 g (5½ oz/1 bunch) asparagus, trimmed

60 ml (2 fl oz/¼ cup) olive oil

1 onion, finely chopped

2 garlic cloves, crushed

1 celery stalk, chopped

1.5 litres (52 fl oz/6 cups) vegetable stock

150 g (5½ oz/1 cup) green peas

80 g (2¾ oz/2 cups) shredded silverbeet (Swiss chard) leaves

PISTOU

3 garlic cloves, peeled

a large handful of basil

80 ml (2½ fl oz/⅓ cup) olive oil

50 g (1¾ oz/½ cup) grated parmesan cheese

1 Chop the zucchini, broccoli, green beans and asparagus into 1 cm (½ inch) pieces and set aside.

2 Heat the olive oil in a large heavy-based saucepan. Sauté the onion, garlic and celery over medium heat for 5 minutes, or until golden. Add the zucchini and broccoli and sauté for a further 5 minutes.

3 Add the stock and bring to the boil. Simmer for 5 minutes, then add the beans, asparagus, peas and silverbeet. Simmer for 5 minutes, or until the vegetables are tender. Season well with sea salt and freshly ground black pepper.

4 To make the pistou, put the garlic and basil in a mortar and pestle or small food processor and crush together. Slowly add the olive oil, and blend to a smooth paste. Stir in the parmesan and season to taste.

5 Ladle the soup into bowls and serve with a dollop of pistou.

ZUCCHINI SOUP

SERVES 4

60 g (2¼ oz) butter
2 large leeks (white part only), thinly sliced
4 garlic cloves, crushed
1.25 kg (2 lb 12 oz) zucchini (courgettes), coarsely grated
1.75 litres (59 fl oz/7 cups) chicken stock
4 tablespoons cream

1   Melt the butter in a saucepan over medium heat. Cook the leek, stirring once or twice, for 2–3 minutes, or until it starts to soften. Reduce the heat to low, add the garlic and cook, covered, stirring once or twice, for 10 minutes, or until the leek is really soft—do not allow it to brown.

2   Add the zucchini to the pan and cook, uncovered, for 4–5 minutes. Pour in the chicken stock and bring to the boil over high heat. Reduce the heat to medium–low and simmer for 20 minutes, or until soft.

3   Let the soup cool slightly and blend half in a blender until smooth. Return to the pan, stir in the cream and gently reheat over medium heat until warmed through. Season to taste with salt and freshly ground black pepper. Serve the soup with crusty fresh bread, if desired.

ORANGE SWEET POTATO SOUP

SERVES 4–6

40 g (1½ oz) butter

2 onions, chopped

2 garlic cloves, crushed

1 kg (2 lb 4 oz) orange sweet potato, peeled and chopped

1 large celery stalk, chopped

1 large green apple, peeled, cored and chopped

1½ teaspoons ground cumin

2 litres (70 fl oz/8 cups) chicken stock

125 g (4½ oz/½ cup) thick natural yoghurt

lavash bread, to serve (optional)

1 Melt the butter in a large pan over low heat. Add the onion and cook, stirring occasionally, for 10 minutes, or until soft. Add the garlic, sweet potato, celery, apple and 1 teaspoon of the cumin and continue to cook for 5–7 minutes, or until well coated. Add the chicken stock and the remaining cumin and bring to the boil over high heat. Reduce the heat and simmer for 25–30 minutes, or until the sweet potato is very soft.

2 Cool the soup slightly and blend in batches until smooth. Return to the cleaned pan and gently stir over medium heat until warmed through. Season with salt and freshly ground black pepper. Divide among serving bowls and top each serve with a dollop of yoghurt.

3 Cut the lavash bread into rectangular strips, brush lightly with oil and place on a baking tray. Bake in a 190°C (375°F/Gas 5) oven for 15–20 minutes, or until crisp and lightly golden. Serve with the soup.

COUNTRY-STYLE VEGETABLE SOUP

SERVES 6

225 g (8 oz/1 cup) soup mix or
  pearl barley

2 teaspoons canola or olive oil

1 large onion, finely chopped

1 green capsicum (pepper), chopped

2 zucchini (courgettes), sliced

2 celery stalks, sliced

125 g (4½ oz) button mushrooms, sliced

2 carrots, sliced

1 orange sweet potato, peeled and
  chopped

375 g (13 oz) pumpkin, peeled
  and chopped

2 litres (70 fl oz/8 cups) vegetable stock

1 **Put the soup mix or barley** in a large bowl, cover with water and leave to soak for 8 hours, or overnight. Drain and rinse well.

2 **Heat the oil in a large saucepan** and cook the onion for 5 minutes, or until soft. Add the capsicum, zucchini, celery and mushrooms and cook for 5 minutes, or until starting to become soft. Add the carrot, sweet potato, pumpkin and soup mix and stir well.

3 **Pour in the stock** and bring to the boil. Reduce the heat to low, partially cover the pan with a lid and simmer for 45 minutes, or until the vegetables and soup mix are just soft. For a thinner soup add a little water.

Note: The soup will keep for 2 days in the refrigerator or in the freezer for 1 month. Bring to the boil before serving. Soup mix is a combination of pearl barley, split peas and lentils. Both pearl barley and soup mix are readily available from supermarkets.

CHICKPEA SOUP WITH SPICED PITTA BREAD

SERVES 4–6

1 tablespoon olive oil

1 large onion, chopped

5 garlic cloves, chopped

1 large carrot, chopped

1 bay leaf

2 celery stalks, chopped

1 teaspoon ground cumin

½ teaspoon ground cinnamon

3 x 425 g (15 oz) tinned chickpeas, drained and rinsed

1.25 litres (44 fl oz/5 cups) chicken stock

1 tablespoon finely chopped flat-leaf (Italian) parsley, plus extra, to garnish

1 tablespoon finely chopped coriander (cilantro) leaves

2 tablespoons lemon juice

extra virgin olive oil, to drizzle

SPICED PITTA BREAD

40 g (1½ oz) butter

2 tablespoons olive oil

2 garlic cloves, crushed

⅛ teaspoon ground cumin

⅛ teaspoon ground cinnamon

⅛ teaspoon cayenne pepper

½ teaspoon sea salt

4 small pitta breads, split

1 Heat the oil in a large saucepan and cook the onion over medium heat for 3–4 minutes, or until soft. Add the garlic, carrot, bay leaf and celery and cook for 4 minutes, or until the vegetables start to caramelize.

2 Stir in the cumin and cinnamon and cook for 1 minute. Add the chickpeas, stock and 1 litre (35 fl oz/4 cups) water and bring to the boil. Reduce the heat and simmer for 1 hour. Allow to cool.

3 Remove the bay leaf and purée the soup. Return to the cleaned pan and stir over medium heat until warmed. Stir in the herbs and lemon juice. Season. Drizzle with oil and garnish with parsley.

4 To make the spiced pitta bread, melt the butter and oil in a saucepan over medium heat. Add the garlic, spices and salt and cook for 1 minute. Place the pitta (smooth side up) on a lined tray and grill (broil) for 1–2 minutes, or until golden. Turn and brush with the spiced butter. Grill until golden and serve with the soup.

CABBAGE SOUP

SERVES 4

100 g (3½ oz/½ cup) dried haricot beans

125 g (4½ oz) bacon, cubed

40 g (1½ oz) butter

1 carrot, sliced

1 onion, chopped

1 leek, white part only, roughly chopped

1 turnip, peeled and chopped

bouquet garni

1.25 litres (44 fl oz/5 cups) chicken stock

400 g (14 oz) white cabbage, finely shredded

1 **Soak the beans** overnight in cold water. Drain, put in a saucepan and cover with cold water. Bring to the boil and simmer for 5 minutes, then drain. Put the bacon in the same saucepan, cover with water and simmer for 5 minutes. Drain and pat dry with paper towels.

2 **Melt the butter** in a large heavy-based saucepan, add the bacon and cook for 5 minutes, without browning. Add the beans, carrot, onion, leek and turnip and cook for 5 minutes. Add the bouquet garni and chicken stock and bring to the boil. Cover and simmer for 30 minutes. Add the cabbage, uncover and simmer for 30 minutes, or until the beans are tender. Remove the bouquet garni before serving and season to taste.

MINESTRONE

SERVES 6

200 g (7 oz./1 cup) dried borlotti beans

50 g (1¾ oz) lard or butter

1 large onion, finely chopped

1 garlic clove, finely chopped

15 g (½ oz) parsley, finely chopped

2 sage leaves

100 g (3½ oz) pancetta or bacon, cubed

2 celery stalks, halved then sliced

2 carrots, sliced

3 potatoes, peeled but left whole

1 teaspoon tomato paste (concentrated purée)

400 g (14 oz) tinned chopped tomatoes

8 basil leaves

3 litres (102 fl oz/12 cups) vegetable stock

2 zucchini (courgettes), sliced

210 g (7½ oz/1⅓ cups) shelled peas

115 g (4 oz) runner beans, cut into 4 cm (1½ inch) lengths

¼ cabbage, shredded

150 g (5½ oz) ditalini, or other small pasta

grated parmesan cheese, to serve

PESTO

2 garlic cloves, crushed

50 g (1¾ oz/⅓ cup) pine nuts

80 g (2¾ oz) basil leaves

4 tablespoons grated parmesan cheese

150 ml (5 fl oz) extra virgin olive oil

1 **Put the dried** borlotti beans in a large bowl, cover with cold water and leave to soak overnight. Drain and rinse under cold water.

2 **Melt the lard** in a large saucepan and add the onion, garlic, parsley, sage and pancetta. Cook over low heat, stirring once or twice, for 10 minutes, or until the onion is soft and golden.

3 **Add the celery,** carrot and potatoes and cook for 5 minutes. Stir in the tomato paste, tomato, basil and dried beans. Season with plenty of pepper. Add the stock and bring slowly to the boil. Cover and leave to simmer for 2 hours, stirring once or twice.

4 **If the potatoes** haven't already broken up, roughly break them up with a fork against the side of the pan. Taste for seasoning and add the zucchini, peas, runner beans, cabbage and pasta. Simmer until the pasta is al dente.

5 **Meanwhile,** to make the pesto, place the garlic, pine nuts, basil and Parmesan in a food processor and mix to a paste. Alternatively, use a mortar and pestle. Add the oil in a steady stream, mixing continuously. Season to taste. Serve the soup with a dollop of pesto and the parmesan.

RED LENTIL, BURGHUL AND MINT SOUP

SERVES 4–6

2 tablespoons olive oil

1 large red onion, finely chopped

2 garlic cloves, crushed

2 tablespoons tomato paste (concentrated purée)

2 tomatoes, finely chopped

2 teaspoons paprika

1 teaspoon cayenne pepper

500 g (17 fl oz/2 cups) red lentils

50 g (1¾ oz/¼ cup) long-grain rice

2.125 litres (74 fl oz/8½ cups) chicken stock

45 g (1½ oz/¼ cup) fine burghul (bulgar wheat)

2 tablespoons chopped mint

2 tablespoons chopped flat-leaf (Italian) parsley

90 g (3¼ oz/⅓ cup) thick natural yoghurt

¼ preserved lemon, pulp removed, zest washed and julienned

1 **Heat the oil** in a saucepan over medium heat. Add the onion and garlic and cook for 2–3 minutes, or until soft. Stir in the tomato paste, tomato and spices and cook for 1 minute.

2 **Add the lentils,** rice and chicken stock, then cover and bring to the boil over high heat. Reduce the heat and simmer for 30–35 minutes, or until the rice is cooked.

3 **Stir in** the burghul and herbs, then season to taste. Divide the soup among serving bowls, garnish with yoghurt and preserved lemon and serve immediately.

Note: This soup will thicken on standing, so if reheating you may need to add more liquid.

TOMATO AND CAPSICUM SOUP WITH POLENTA

SERVES 4

2 tablespoons vegetable oil

2 tablespoons olive oil

2 red onions, finely chopped

2 garlic cloves, crushed

1 tablespoon ground cumin

¼ teaspoon ground cayenne pepper

2 teaspoons paprika

2 red capsicums (peppers), diced

90 g (3¼ oz/⅓ cup) tomato paste (concentrated purée)

250 ml (9 fl oz/1 cup) dry white wine

800 g (1 lb 12 oz) tinned chopped tomatoes

2 long red chillies, seeded and chopped

500 ml (17 fl oz/2 cups) chicken or vegetable stock

3 tablespoons chopped flat-leaf (Italian) parsley

4 tablespoons chopped coriander (cilantro) leaves

POLENTA AND OLIVE STICKS

500 ml (17 fl oz/2 cups) vegetable stock

185 g (6½ oz/1¼ cups) coarse polenta

100 g (3½ oz) pitted Kalamata olives, chopped

125 ml (4 fl oz/½ cup) olive oil

1 Heat the oils in a large saucepan over medium heat and cook the onion and garlic for 2–3 minutes, or until soft.

2 Reduce the heat to low, add the spices and cook for 1–2 minutes. Add the capsicum and cook for 5 minutes. Stir in the tomato paste and wine, simmer for 2 minutes, or until reduced slightly. Add the tomato, chilli, stock and 500 ml (2 cups) water. Season. Simmer for 20 minutes. Purée the soup with the herbs.

3 To make the polenta and olive sticks, grease a 20 x 30 cm (8 x 12 inch) shallow baking tray. Bring the stock and 500 ml (17 fl oz/2 cups) water to the boil in a saucepan. Slowly add the polenta in a fine stream, whisking until smooth. Reduce the heat to low. Cook, stirring constantly, for 15–20 minutes, or until it starts to come away from the side. Stir in the olives, then spoon into the tray, smoothing the surface. Cover and chill for 30 minutes, or until firm. Cut into sticks.

4 Heat the oil in a large deep frying pan to 190°C (375°F), or until a cube of bread browns in 10 seconds. Cook the sticks in batches on each side for 1–2 minutes, or until crisp. Drain well, and serve with the soup.

FRENCH ONION SOUP

SERVES 6

50 g (1¾ oz) butter

750 g (1 lb 10 oz) onions, finely sliced

2 garlic cloves, finely chopped

45 g (1½ oz/⅓ cup) plain (all-purpose) flour

2 litres (70 fl oz/8 cups) beef or chicken stock

250 ml (9 fl oz/1 cup) white wine

1 bay leaf

2 thyme sprigs

12 slices stale baguette

100 g (3½ oz) gruyère cheese, finely grated

1 **Melt the butter** in a heavy-based saucepan and add the onion. Cook over low heat, stirring occasionally, for 25 minutes, or until the onion is deep golden brown and beginning to caramelize.

2 **Add the garlic** and flour and stir continuously for 2 minutes. Gradually blend in the stock and the wine, stirring all the time, and bring to the boil. Add the bay leaf and thyme and season. Cover the pan and simmer for 25 minutes. Remove the bay leaf and thyme and check the seasoning. Preheat the grill (broiler).

3 **Toast the baguette** slices, then divide among six warmed soup bowls and ladle the soup over the top. Sprinkle with the grated cheese and grill (broil) until the cheese melts and turns light golden brown. Serve immediately.

WATERCRESS SOUP

SERVES 4

30 g (1 oz) butter

1 onion, finely chopped

250 g (9 oz) potatoes, diced

625 ml (2½ oz/2½ cups) chicken stock

1 kg (2 lb 4 oz) watercress, trimmed
    and chopped

125 ml (4 fl oz/½ cup) cream

125 ml (4 fl oz/½ cup) milk

freshly grated nutmeg

2 tablespoons chopped chives

1 **Melt the butter** in a large saucepan and add the onion. Cover the pan and cook over low heat until the onion is softened but not brown. Add the potato and chicken stock and simmer for 12 minutes, or until the potato is tender. Add the watercress and cook for 1 minute.

2 **Remove from the heat** and leave the soup to cool a little before pouring into a blender or food processor. Blend until smooth and return to the cleaned saucepan.

3 **Bring the soup** gently back to the boil and stir in the cream and milk. Season with nutmeg, salt and pepper and reheat without boiling. Serve garnished with chives.

SOUTH AMERICAN BLACK BEAN SOUP

SERVES 4

330 g (11½ oz/1½ cups) black turtle beans (black kidney beans)
1 tablespoon vegetable oil
1 onion, finely chopped
1 leek, finely chopped
2 garlic cloves, crushed
2 teaspoons ground cumin
4 bacon slices, diced
1 litre (35 fl oz/4 cups) chicken stock
90 g (3¼ oz/⅓ cup) sour cream
1½ tablespoons snipped chives

1 **Soak** the black beans in a bowl of cold water overnight. Drain well.

2 **Heat the oil** in a large saucepan over medium heat and cook the onion, leek, garlic and cumin for about 3 minutes, or until soft. Add the bacon and cook for 2–3 minutes, or until lightly browned.

3 **Add the black beans,** chicken stock and 500 ml (17 fl oz/ 2 cups) water to the saucepan and bring to the boil over high heat. Reduce the heat and simmer for 1 hour, or until the black beans are tender. Season with salt and freshly ground black pepper.

4 **Cool slightly** and blend half the soup in batches in a blender until smooth. Return to the saucepan and stir through the unblended soup. Spoon into bowls, dollop with sour cream and garnish with the chives.

UDON NOODLE AND MUSHROOM SOUP

SERVES 4

1.5 litres (52 fl oz/6 cups)
   vegetable stock

2 tablespoons mirin

2 teaspoons grated fresh ginger

1 teaspoon wakame (dried seaweed)
   flakes

150 g (5½ oz) fresh shiitake
   mushrooms, sliced

440 g (15½ oz) packet fresh udon
   noodles

2 spring onions (scallions),
   sliced diagonally

75 g (2½ oz) snow peas (mangetout),
   trimmed and finely sliced lengthways

50 g (1¾ oz) bean sprouts, trimmed

2 tablespoons light soy sauce

1 nori sheet, shredded

1 tablespoon shichimi togarashi, for
   sprinkling

1   Put the stock in a large saucepan and bring to the boil. Reduce the heat to a simmer. Add the mirin, ginger, wakame and sliced mushrooms. Simmer for 5 minutes.

2   Put the noodles in a large bowl and pour over boiling water. Leave for 1 minute to heat through. Drain, refresh under cold running water and separate the noodles, then set aside.

3   Add the spring onions, snow peas, bean sprouts, soy sauce and shredded nori to the stock and simmer for a further 2 minutes.

4   Divide the noodles among four large serving bowls. Ladle over the hot broth and vegetables. Sprinkle with the shichimi togarashi.

LENTIL AND SILVERBEET SOUP

SERVES 6

CHICKEN STOCK

1 kg (2 lb 8 oz) chicken trimmings (neck, ribs, wings), fat removed

1 small onion, roughly chopped

1 bay leaf

3–4 flat-leaf (Italian) parsley sprigs

1–2 oregano or thyme sprigs

280 g (10 oz) brown lentils

850 g (1 lb 14 oz) silverbeet (Swiss chard)

3 tablespoons olive oil

1 large onion, finely chopped

4 garlic cloves, crushed

25 g (1 oz) coriander (cilantro) leaves, finely chopped

4 tablespoons lemon juice

lemon wedges, to serve

1 To make the stock, put all the ingredients in a large saucepan. Add 3 litres (102 fl oz/12 cups) of water and bring to the boil. Skim any scum from the surface. Reduce the heat and simmer for 2 hours. Strain the stock, discarding the trimmings, onion and herbs. Chill overnight. You will need about 1 litre (35 fl oz/4 cups).

2 Skim any fat from the stock. Put the lentils in a large saucepan, add the stock and 1 litre (35 fl oz/4 cups) of water. Bring to the boil, then reduce the heat and simmer, covered, for 1 hour.

3 Meanwhile, remove the stems from the silverbeet and shred the leaves. Heat the oil in a saucepan over medium heat and cook the onion for 2–3 minutes, or until transparent. Add the garlic and cook for 1 minute. Add the silverbeet and toss for 2–3 minutes, or until wilted. Stir the mixture into the lentils. Add the coriander and lemon juice, season, and simmer, covered for 15–20 minutes. Serve with lemon wedges.

PUMPKIN SOUP

SERVES 4

2 kg (4 lb 8 oz) butternut
pumpkin (squash)

40 g (1½ oz) butter

2 onions, chopped

½ teaspoon cumin seeds

1 litre (35 fl oz/4 cups) chicken stock

1 bay leaf

4 tablespoons cream

pinch nutmeg

1 **Peel the pumpkin** and chop into small chunks. Melt the butter in a large saucepan, add the onion and cook over low heat for 5–7 minutes, or until soft. Add the cumin seeds and cook for 1 minute, then add the pumpkin pieces, stock and bay leaf. Increase the heat to high and bring to the boil, then reduce the heat and simmer for 20 minutes, or until the pumpkin is soft. Remove the bay leaf and allow the soup to cool slightly.

2 **Blend the soup** in batches until it is smooth. Return to the cleaned pan and stir in the cream and nutmeg. Simmer gently until warmed through and season with salt and freshly ground black pepper before serving.

CAULIFLOWER AND ALMOND SOUP WITH HOT CHEESE ROLLS

SERVES 4

75 g (2½ oz/½ cup) blanched almonds

1 tablespoon olive oil

1 large leek, white part only, chopped

2 garlic cloves, crushed

1 kg (2 lb 4 oz) cauliflower, cut into small florets

2 desiree potatoes, cut into 1.5 cm (5/8 inch) pieces

1.75 litres (59 fl oz/7 cups) chicken stock

CHEESE ROLLS

4 round bread rolls

40 g (1½ oz) softened butter

125 g (4½ oz) cheddar cheese, grated

50 g (1¾ oz) parmesan cheese, grated

1 **Preheat the oven** to 180°C (350°F/Gas 4). Place the almonds on a baking tray and toast for 5 minutes, or until golden.

2 **Heat the oil** in a large saucepan over medium heat and cook the leek for 2–3 minutes, or until softened. Add the garlic and cook for 30 seconds, then add the cauliflower, potato and stock. Bring to the boil, then reduce the heat and simmer for 15 minutes, or until the vegetables are very tender. Cool for 5 minutes.

3 **Blend the soup** with the almonds in batches in a blender until smooth. Season to taste with salt and pepper. Return to the cleaned pan and stir over medium heat until heated through. Serve with the cheese rolls, if desired.

4 **To make the cheese rolls,** split the rolls and butter both sides. Combine the grated cheeses and divide evenly among the rolls. Sandwich together and wrap in foil. Bake in the oven for 15–20 minutes, or until the cheese has melted.

BEAN AND BARLEY SOUP

SERVES 4

200 g (7 oz) dried borlotti beans

2 tablespoons olive oil

1 small onion, thinly sliced

2 garlic cloves, crushed

1.5 litres (52 fl oz/6 cups) chicken stock

1 tablespoon finely chopped thyme
   or sage

200 g (7 oz) pearl barley

100 g (3½ oz) parmesan cheese, grated

1 tablespoon finely chopped parsley

4 teaspoons extra virgin olive oil

1 Soak the borlotti beans in cold water overnight. Drain off the water and put the beans in a large saucepan with plenty of cold water. Bring to the boil and simmer until tender (this will take about 1½ hours depending on the age of the beans—older drier beans may take longer to soften). Drain.

2 Heat the olive oil in a large saucepan and cook the onion over low heat for 6 minutes, or until soft. Season with salt and pepper. Add the garlic and cook without browning for 20–30 seconds. Add the stock and thyme or sage and bring to the boil.

3 Stir in the barley a little at a time so that the stock continues to boil, then lower the heat and simmer for 15 minutes. Add the borlotti beans and simmer for 30 minutes, or until the barley is tender and the soup is thick.

4 Purée one-third of the soup until smooth, leaving the remainder unpuréed to give the soup a little texture. Return to the saucepan and stir in the Parmesan and parsley. Season and stir in 125–250 ml (4–9 fl oz) hot water to give a spoonable consistency. Serve immediately, with a teaspoon of extra virgin olive oil stirred through each bowl.

Note: If you need to make this soup quickly or you have forgotten to soak the dried beans overnight, use tinned borlotti beans instead. They don't need soaking or pre-cooking, simply rinse them well and add them to the barley when it is almost cooked.

RAMEN NOODLES WITH SOY BROTH

SERVES 4

BROTH

1 kg (2 lb 4 oz) pork bones

1 kg (2 lb 4 oz) chicken bones

10 spring onions (scallions), bruised

10 cm (4 inch) fresh ginger piece, sliced

1 bulb garlic, cut in half through the centre

2 carrots, peeled and chopped

10 cm (4 inch) konbu (kelp) square piece, wiped with a damp cloth

125–185 ml (4–6 fl oz/½–¾ cup) shoyu (Japanese soy sauce)

80 ml (2½ fl oz/⅓ cup) sake

8 dried shiitake mushrooms

500 g (1 lb 2 oz) fresh ramen noodles

100 g (3½ oz) bamboo shoots, sliced

125 g (4½ oz) Chinese barbecued pork, sliced

200 g (7 oz) bok choy (pak choy), sliced lengthways into wide strips, blanched

50 g (1¾ oz) bean sprouts, blanched

4 spring onions (scallions), cut into 4 cm (1½ in) lengths

shichimi togarashi (seven-spice mix) to serve, optional

chilli sesame oil to serve, optional

1 **To make the broth,** put the pork and chicken bones in a stockpot or large, deep saucepan and cover with cold water. Bring to the boil over high heat, then drain. Rinse the bones, then return them to a clean stockpot. Add the spring onions, ginger, garlic, carrot and konbu and pour in enough cold water to cover by about 5 cm (2 in). Bring to the boil over high heat, remove the konbu, then reduce to a simmer, skimming any scum off the surface. Cook, uncovered, for 6 hours, or until the liquid has reduced to about 1.5 litres (52 fl oz/6 cups). Cool slightly, remove the bones, then pour the stock through a fine strainer. Refrigerate for 6 hours, or until cold.

2 **Meanwhile,** soak the shiitake in hot water for 30 minutes, then drain well. Discard the stems.

3 **Bring a large saucepan of lightly salted water** to the boil, add the noodles and separate with chopsticks. Cook for 1–2 minutes, or until tender. Drain well, then rinse under cold running water, rubbing the noodles together lightly with your hands to remove any excess starch.

4 **Scoop off any fat** from the surface of the cooled broth, then pour the broth into a large saucepan. Add the shoyu and sake, bring to the boil over high heat, then reduce to a simmer. Pour a little broth into four large warmed bowls, then divide the noodles among the bowls. Ladle the broth over the noodles so that it just comes to the top of the noodles. Using chopsticks, neatly arrange small piles of the shiitake, bamboo shoots, pork, bok choy, bean sprouts and spring onion on top of the noodles. If you like, sprinkle with shichimi togarashi and drizzle with a little chilli sesame oil. Freeze any leftover broth for next time.

LA RIBOLLITA

SERVES 4

4 tablespoons olive oil

1 onion, finely chopped

1 large carrot

3 celery stalks

2 garlic cloves, crushed

250 g (9 oz) cavolo nero or savoy cabbage

1 zucchini (courgette), finely chopped

400 g (14 oz) cooked cannellini or borlotti beans

400 g (14 oz) tinned peeled tomatoes

1 whole dried chilli

200 ml (7 fl oz) red wine

1 litre (35 fl oz/4 cups) chicken stock

75 g (2½ oz) stale country-style bread, such as ciabatta or pugliese, crusts removed and broken into 2.5 cm (1⁄16 inch) pieces

extra virgin olive oil, to serve

1 To make the soffritto (base flavouring), pour the oil into a large saucepan and first add the onion. Cook the onion gently over low heat. While the onion is cooking, finely chop the carrot and celery and add them to the saucepan as you go along. Add the garlic, then leave to cook for a few minutes.

2 Strip the leaves of the cavolo nero from the stems or cut away the thick stem of the savoy cabbage. Wash and finely chop the stems and roughly chop the leaves. Add the cabbage stems and courgette to the soffritto and cook, stirring occasionally, for about 5 minutes, or until the vegetables are translucent and have soaked up some of the olive oil.

3 Stir in the beans and cook for 5 minutes more, then add the tomatoes and chilli and cook for a further 5 minutes to reduce the liquid.

4 Add the cabbage leaves and mix into the soup, stirring until just wilted. Add the wine and stock and simmer for 40 minutes.

5 Add the bread to the pan (if the bread is fresh, cut it into the pieces and then dry it out a little in the oven first to stop it disintegrating into the soup). Mix briefly and remove the pan from the heat. Leave for about 30 minutes to rest the soup and let the flavours mingle. Serve hot but not boiling with a generous drizzle of extra virgin olive oil (you may want to remove the chilli before you serve the soup).

Note: Don't stir it too much or the bread will break up and alter the texture of the soup. Leave to cool for 5 minutes before serving in cold bowls. Ribollita should be served warm, rather than piping hot.

CHICKPEA AND HERB DUMPLING SOUP

SERVES 4

1 tablespoon oil

1 onion, chopped

2 garlic cloves, crushed

2 teaspoons ground cumin

1 teaspoon ground coriander

¼ teaspoon chilli powder

600 g (1 lb 5 oz) tinned chickpeas, drained

875 ml (30 fl oz/3½ cups) vegetable stock

800 g (1lb 12 oz) tinned chopped tomatoes

1 tablespoon chopped coriander (cilantro) leaves

DUMPLINGS

125 g (4½ oz/1 cup) self-raising flour

25 g (1 oz) butter, chopped

2 tablespoons grated parmesan cheese

2 tablespoons mixed chopped herbs (chives, flat-leaf (Italian) parsley and coriander (cilantro) leaves)

60 ml (2 fl oz/¼ cup) full-cream (whole) milk

crusty bread, to serve

1   Heat the oil in a large saucepan and cook the onion over medium heat for 2–3 minutes, or until soft. Add the garlic, cumin, ground coriander and chilli, and cook for 1 minute, or until fragrant. Add the chickpeas, stock and tomato. Bring to the boil, then reduce the heat and simmer, covered, for 10 minutes. Stir in the coriander leaves.

2   To make the dumplings, sift the flour into a bowl and add the chopped butter. Rub the butter into the flour with your fingertips until it resembles fine breadcrumbs. Stir in the parmesan and mixed fresh herbs. Make a well in the centre, add the milk and mix with a flat-bladed knife until just combined. Bring the dough together into a rough ball, divide into eight portions and roll into small balls.

3   Add the dumplings to the soup, cover and simmer for 20 minutes, or until a skewer comes out clean when inserted into the centre of the dumplings. Serve with cracked black pepper and crusty bread.

SOUPE AU PISTOU

SERVES 4

250 g (9 oz) dried haricot beans

2 teaspoons olive oil

1 onion, finely chopped

2 garlic cloves, crushed

1 celery stalk, chopped

3 carrots, diced

1 bouquet garni

4 all-purpose potatoes, diced

150 g (5½ oz) green beans
  small, chopped

500 ml (17 fl oz/2 cups) chicken stock

3 tomatoes

4 zucchini (courgettes), diced

150 g (5½ oz) vermicelli noodles, broken
  into pieces

150 g (5½ oz), fresh or frozen peas

PISTOU

6 garlic cloves, peeled and chopped

80 g (2¾ oz) basil

100 g (3½ oz) parmesan cheese, grated

200 ml (7 fl oz) olive oil

1 Soak the haricot beans in cold water overnight. Drain, then put in a saucepan and cover with cold water. Bring to the boil, then lower the heat and simmer for 1 hour, or until the beans are tender. Drain well.

2 To make the pistou, put the garlic, basil and parmesan in a mortar and pestle or food processor and pound or process until finely ground. Slowly add the olive oil, pounding constantly with the mortar and pestle. If you are using a food processor, add the oil in a thin stream with the motor running. Mix thoroughly. Cover with plastic wrap and set aside.

3 Heat the olive oil in a large saucepan. Add the onion and garlic and cook over low heat for 5 minutes, or until softened but not browned. Add the celery, carrot and bouquet garni and cook for 10 minutes, stirring occasionally. Add the potato, green beans, chicken stock and 1.75 litres (61 fl oz/7 cups) water and simmer for 10 minutes.

4 Score a cross in the base of each tomato. Plunge into boiling water for 20 seconds, then drain and peel the skin away from the cross. Chop the tomatoes finely, discarding the cores. Add to the soup with the courgettes, haricot beans, vermicelli and peas. Cook for 10 minutes or until tender (if you are using frozen peas, add them at the last minute just to heat through). Season and serve with pistou spooned on top.

SPINACH SOUP

SERVES 4

30 g (1 oz) butter

1 onion, finely chopped

500 g (1 lb 2 oz) floury potatoes, grated

1 litre (35 fl oz/4 cups) vegetable stock

500 g (1 lb 2 oz) frozen chopped
English spinach

¼ teaspoon ground nutmeg

sour cream, to serve

1   Melt the butter in a large saucepan over medium heat. Add the chopped onion and cook, stirring occasionally, until soft but not browned.

2   Add the potato and stock to the pan and mix well, scraping the onion from the bottom of the pan. Add the unthawed blocks of spinach and cook, covered, until the spinach has thawed and broken up, stirring occasionally. Uncover and simmer, stirring often, for 10–15 minutes, or until the potato is very soft. Transfer to a blender or food processor and blend in batches until smooth.

3   Return the soup to the pan and gently reheat. Add the nutmeg and season. Serve with sour cream swirled on top.

MUSHROOM SOUP

SERVES 4

40 g (1½ oz) butter

1 onion, finely chopped

12 large (about 1.4 kg/3 lb 3 oz) field
  mushrooms, finely chopped

2 garlic cloves, crushed

2 tablespoons dry sherry

1 litre (35 fl oz/4 cups) vegetable or
  chicken stock

2 tablespoons flat-leaf (Italian) parsley,
  finely chopped

cream, to serve

1 Melt the butter in a large saucepan and fry the onion until the onion is translucent but not browned.

2 Add the mushroom and garlic and continue frying. The mushrooms might give off a lot of liquid, so fry for 15–20 minutes, or until it is all absorbed back into the mixture.

3 Add the sherry to the pan, increase the heat and let the mixture bubble—this burns off the alcohol but leaves the flavour. Cool slightly, then transfer to a blender. Process until a smooth paste forms, then add the stock and blend until smooth. Add a couple of tablespoons of cream and blend together. Pour back into the saucepan and heat gently. Garnish with the parsley.

SERVES 6

200 g (7 oz) day-old white crusty bread, crusts removed

150 g (5½ oz/1 cup) whole blanched almonds

3–4 garlic cloves, chopped

125 ml (4 fl oz/½ cup) extra virgin olive oil, plus 2 tablespoons, extra

80 ml (2½ fl oz/⅓ cup) sherry or white wine vinegar

325–375 ml (11–13 fl oz/ 1¼–1½ cups) vegetable stock

sea salt, to season

80 g (2¾ oz) day-old white crusty bread, crusts removed and cut into 1 cm (½ inch) cubes

200 g (7 oz) small seedless green grapes

1 Soak the bread in cold water for 5 minutes, then squeeze out any excess liquid. Put the almonds and garlic in a food processor and process until ground. Add the bread and process until smooth.

2 With the motor running, add the oil in a steady slow stream until the mixture is the consistency of thick mayonnaise (add a little water if the mixture is too thick). Slowly add the sherry or vinegar and 325 ml (11 fl oz/ 1¼ cups) of the stock. Blend for 1 minute. Season with sea salt. Refrigerate for at least 2 hours. The soup thickens on refrigeration so you may need to add stock or water to thin it.

3 When ready to serve, heat the extra oil in a frying pan, add the extra bread cubes and toss over medium heat for 2–3 minutes, or until golden. Drain on paper towels. Serve the soup very cold. Garnish with the grapes and bread cubes.

SPRING VEGETABLE SOUP WITH BASIL PESTO

SERVES 4

1.25 litres (44 fl oz/5 cups) vegetable or chicken stock

1 tablespoon extra virgin olive oil

8 spring onions (scallions), finely sliced

2 celery stalks, finely sliced

12 baby (dutch) carrots, sliced

310 g (11 oz) asparagus, woody ends removed, cut into 3 cm (1¼ inch) lengths

150 g (5½ oz) baby corn, cut into 3 cm (1¼ inch) lengths

60 g (2¼ oz/¼ cup) fresh or bottled pesto

extra virgin olive oil, to thin pesto (see Note)

shaved parmesan cheese, to garnish

1 **Bring the stock** to the boil in a large saucepan. Meanwhile, heat the olive oil in a large heavy-based saucepan and add the spring onion and celery. Cover and cook over medium heat for 5 minutes, or until softened.

2 **Add the stock** to the spring onion mixture and mix well. Add the carrot, asparagus and corn to the pan. Return the mixture to the boil, then reduce the heat and simmer for 10 minutes.

3 **Top with a dollop** of pesto, season to taste, and garnish with shaved parmesan.

Note: Homemade pesto or fresh pesto from a deli will give a better flavour than bottled pesto. If you prefer a thinner pesto, mix it with a little olive oil to give it a runnier consistency.

BORSCHT

SERVES 6

6 large (1.5 kg/3 lb 5 oz) beetroot, peeled
1½ tablespoons caster (superfine) sugar
125 ml (4 fl oz/½ cup) lemon juice
3 eggs
sour cream, to serve (optional)

1 **Grate the beetroot,** and put in a saucepan with the caster sugar and 2.25 litres (76 fl oz/9 cups) water. Stir over low heat until the sugar has dissolved. Simmer, partially covered, for about 30 minutes, skimming the surface occasionally.

2 **Add the lemon juice** and simmer, uncovered, for 10 minutes. Remove the pan from the heat.

3 **Whisk the eggs** in a bowl. Gradually pour the eggs into the beetroot mixture, whisking constantly and taking care not to curdle the eggs. Season to taste. Allow the soup to cool, then cover and refrigerate until cold. Served with a dollop of sour cream, if desired.

GREEN CURRY VEGETABLE SOUP

SERVES 6

2 teaspoons peanut oil

1 tablespoon green curry paste

3 kaffir lime leaves

1.25 litres (44 fl oz/5 cups) vegetable or
chicken stock

670 ml (23 fl oz/2⅔ cups) coconut milk

600 g (1 lb 5 oz) butternut pumpkin
(squash), cut into 1.5 cm (5/8 inch)
cubes

250 g (9 oz) small yellow squash
(pattypan squash), sliced

115 g (4 oz) fresh baby corn spears,
halved lengthways

2 tablespoons mushroom soy sauce

2 tablespoons lime juice

1 teaspoon sugar

1½ tablespoons Vietnamese mint,
finely chopped

1 Heat the oil in a large saucepan and add the curry paste
and lime leaves. Cook, stirring, over medium heat for
1 minute, or until fragrant.

2 Bring the stock to the boil in a separate saucepan.

3 Gradually add the stock and coconut milk to the curry
mixture and bring to the boil. Add the pumpkin, squash and
corn, and simmer over low heat for 12 minutes, or until the
pumpkin is tender.

4 Add the soy sauce and lime juice, and season to taste
with sugar, salt and black pepper. Garnish with the mint
before serving.

MUSHROOM AND TORTELLINI SOUP

SERVES 4

1 tablespoon olive oil
175 g (6 oz) small flat mushrooms, sliced
6 spring onions (scallions), sliced
1 small garlic clove, crushed
1.25 litres (44 fl oz/5 cups) vegetable or chicken stock
1 tablespoon port
2 teaspoons Worcestershire sauce
200 g (7 oz) fresh large ricotta tortellini
shaved parmesan cheese, to garnish

1 **Heat the oil** in a large heavy-based saucepan over high heat. Add the mushrooms and cook for 2 minutes, browning the mushrooms before turning. Add the spring onion and garlic and cook for a further 1 minute.

2 **Meanwhile,** bring the stock to the boil in a separate saucepan. Add the stock, port and Worcestershire sauce to the mushroom mixture and bring to the boil. Add the tortellini and simmer for 8 minutes, or until the tortellini is al dente.

3 **Season to taste** and serve topped with shaved parmesan.

BROTH WITH RAVIOLI

SERVES 2

1.5 litres (52 fl oz/6 cups) vegetable or chicken stock

500 g (1 lb 2 oz) spinach and ricotta ravioli

175 g (6 oz) snowpeas (mangetout), sliced on the diagonal

4 tablespoons chopped flat-leaf (Italian) parsley

4 tablespoons chopped basil

grated parmesan cheese, to garnish

1 **Place the stock** in a large heavy-based saucepan and bring to the boil. Add the ravioli and cook for 8–10 minutes, or until the pasta is al dente.

2 **Season to taste** and stir in the snowpeas, parsley and basil. Sprinkle with grated parmesan just before serving.

CAPSICUM, SPINACH AND CHICKPEA SOUP

SERVES 4

1 tablespoon olive oil

8 spring onions (scallions), finely sliced

1 red capsicum (pepper)

1 garlic clove, crushed

1 teaspoon cumin seeds

375 ml (13 fl oz/1½ cups) tomato passata (puréed tomatoes)

750 ml (26 fl oz/3 cups) vegetable or beef stock

300 g (10½ oz) tinned chickpeas, rinsed and drained

2 teaspoons red wine vinegar

1–2 teaspoons sugar

100 g (3½ oz) baby English spinach leaves

1 **Heat the oil** in a large heavy-based saucepan over medium heat and stir in the spring onion. Reduce the heat and cook, covered, for 2–3 minutes, or until softened.

2 **Remove the seeds** and membrane from the capsicum and finely dice. Add the capsicum, garlic and cumin seeds to the pan and cook for 1 minute.

3 **Add the passata** and stock and bring the mixture to the boil. Reduce the heat and simmer for 10 minutes. Add the chickpeas, vinegar and sugar to the soup and simmer for a further 5 minutes. Stir in the baby spinach and season to taste. Cook until the spinach begins to wilt. Serve immediately.

CHICKPEA, POTATO AND SPINACH SOUP

SERVES 4

1 litre (35 fl oz/4 cups) vegetable stock

1½ tablespoons olive oil

1 onion, finely chopped

1 large potato, cut into 1.5 cm (⅝ inch) cubes

1½ teaspoons paprika

2 garlic cloves, crushed

400 g (14 oz) tinned chickpeas, drained

1 large tomato, cut into small cubes

50 g (1¾ oz) English spinach, coarsely shredded

25 g (1 oz/¼ cup) grated parmesan cheese

1 Put the stock in a saucepan, then cover and slowly bring to the boil.

2 Heat the olive oil in a large heavy-based saucepan. Cook the onion for 2 minutes, or until soft. Add the potato to the onion, and stir in the paprika, garlic and chickpeas. Add the onion mixture to the stock and bring to the boil. Stir in the tomato, and season.

3 Simmer for 10 minutes, or until the potato is tender. Add the spinach and cook until wilted. Top with parmesan and season to taste.

SPICY PARSNIP SOUP

SERVES 6

1.25 litres (44 fl oz/5 cups) vegetable or chicken stock

30 g (1 oz) butter

1 white onion, cut into quarters and finely sliced

1 leek, finely sliced

500 g (1 lb 2 oz) parsnips, peeled and finely sliced

1 tablespoon Madras curry powder

1 teaspoon ground cumin

315 ml (11 oz/1¼ cups) cream (see Note)

10 g (¼ oz/⅓ cup) coriander (cilantro) leaves

1 **Bring the stock to the boil** in a saucepan and keep at a low simmer.

2 **Melt the butter** in a large saucepan over medium heat. Add the onion, leek and parsnip and cook, covered, for 5 minutes. Add the curry powder and cumin and cook for 1 minute. Stir in the stock and cook, covered, over medium heat for about 10 minutes, or until tender.

3 **Transfer the soup** to a blender or food processor and blend in batches until smooth. Return to the pan. Stir in the cream and warm through over low heat. Season to taste and scatter with coriander leaves.

Note: This soup is also delicious without the cream, if you prefer not to add it.

CHILLI, CORN AND RED CAPSICUM SOUP

SERVES 4

1 coriander (cilantro) sprig

4 sweet corn cobs

30 g (1 oz) butter

2 red capsicums (peppers), diced

1 small onion, finely chopped

1 small red chilli, finely chopped

1 tablespoon plain (all-purpose) flour

500 ml (17 fl oz/2 cups) vegetable stock

125 ml (4 fl oz/½ cup) cream

1 Trim the leaves off the coriander and finely chop the root and stems. Cut the kernels off the corn cobs.

2 Heat the butter in a saucepan over medium heat. Add the corn kernels, capsicum, onion and chilli and stir to coat in the butter. Cook, covered, over low heat, stirring occasionally, for 10 minutes, or until soft. Increase the heat to medium, add the coriander root and stem and cook, stirring, for 30 seconds, or until fragrant. Sprinkle with the flour and stir for 1 minute. Remove from the heat and gradually stir in the stock. Add 500 ml (17 fl oz/2 cups) of water and return to the heat. Bring to the boil, reduce the heat to low and simmer, covered, for 30 minutes, or until the vegetables are tender. Cool slightly.

3 Pour 500 ml (17 fl oz/2 cups) of the soup into a blender and purée until smooth. Return the purée to the soup in the pan, pour in the cream and gently heat until warmed through. Season. Sprinkle with the coriander leaves.

SOBA NOODLE AND VEGETABLE SOUP

SERVES 4

250 g (9 oz) soba noodles

2 dried shiitake mushrooms

2 litres (70 fl oz/8 cups) vegetable stock

120 g (4¼ oz) snowpeas (mangetout), cut into strips

2 small carrots, cut into thin 5 cm (2 inch) strips

2 garlic cloves, finely chopped

6 spring onions (scallions), cut into 5 cm (2 inch) lengths and thinly sliced lengthways

3 cm (1¼ inch) piece ginger, cut into julienne strips

4 tablespoons soy sauce

3 tablespoons mirin or sake

90 g (3¼ oz) bean sprouts, trimmed

coriander (cilantro) leaves, to garnish

---

1 **Cook the noodles** according to the packet instructions. Drain well.

2 **Soak the mushrooms** in 125 ml (4 fl oz/½ cup) of boiling water until soft. Drain, reserving the liquid. Remove the stalk and slice the mushrooms.

3 **Combine the stock,** mushrooms, reserved liquid, snowpeas, carrot, garlic, spring onion and ginger in a large saucepan. Bring slowly to the boil, then reduce the heat to low and simmer for 5 minutes, or until the vegetables are tender. Add the soy sauce, mirin and bean sprouts. Cook for a further 3 minutes.

4 **Divide the noodles** among four large serving bowls. Ladle the hot liquid and vegetables over the top and garnish with coriander.

CARROT AND GINGER SOUP

SERVES 4

750 ml (26 fl oz/3 cups) vegetable stock

1 tablespoon oil

1 onion, chopped

1 tablespoon grated fresh ginger

1 kg (2 lb 4 oz) carrots, chopped

2 tablespoons chopped coriander
(cilantro) leaves

1 Put the stock in a saucepan and bring to the boil.

2 Heat the oil in a large heavy-based saucepan over medium heat. Add the onion and ginger and cook for 2 minutes, or until the onion has softened.

3 Add the stock and carrots. Bring to the boil, then reduce the heat and simmer for 10–15 minutes, or until the carrot is cooked and tender.

4 Pour into a blender or food processor and process in batches until smooth. Return to the pan and add a little more stock or water if needed.

5 Stir in the coriander and season to taste. Heat gently before serving.

COLD SPICY ROAST CAPSICUM SOUP

SERVES 4

4 red capsicums (peppers)
2 teaspoons oil
2 garlic cloves, crushed
4 spring onions (scallions), sliced
1 teaspoon finely chopped seeded chillies
425 g (15 oz) tinned crushed tomatoes
125 ml (4 fl oz/½ cup) chilled vegetable stock
1 teaspoon balsamic vinegar
2 tablespoons chopped basil

1 **Cut the capsicums** into quarters and remove the seeds and membrane. Put the capsicums skin side up under a hot grill (broiler) and grill until the skins blacken and blisters. Cool in a plastic bag, then peel away the skin and roughly chop the flesh.

2 **Heat the oil** in a small saucepan. Add the garlic, spring onion and chilli and cook over low heat for 1–2 minutes, or until softened.

3 **Transfer to a food processor** or blender, and add the capsicum, crushed tomatoes and stock. Blend until smooth, then stir in the vinegar and basil. Season to taste. Refrigerate, then serve cold.

SAFFRON AND JERUSALEM ARTICHOKE SOUP

SERVES 4

1 pinch saffron threads

250 g (9 oz) Jerusalem artichokes

2 tablespoons lemon juice

1 tablespoon olive oil

1 large onion, finely chopped

1 litre (35 fl oz/4 cups) vegetable or chicken stock

3 teaspoons ground cumin

500 g (1 lb 2 oz) desiree potatoes, grated

2 teaspoons lemon juice, extra

1 **Put the saffron** threads in a bowl with 2 tablespoons of boiling water and set aside.

2 **Peel** and thinly slice the artichokes, dropping the slices into a bowl of water mixed with lemon juice to prevent discolouration.

3 **Heat the oil** in a large heavy-based saucepan over medium heat. Add the onion and cook for 2–3 minutes, or until the onion is softened. Bring the stock to the boil in a large saucepan. Add the cumin to the onion mixture and cook for a further 30 seconds, or until fragrant. Add the drained artichokes, potato, saffron mixture, stock and extra lemon juice. Bring to the boil, then reduce the heat and simmer for 15–18 minutes, or until the artichokes are very soft.

4 **Transfer to a blender** and process in batches until smooth. Return the soup to the pan and season to taste. Reheat over medium heat and serve immediately.

SPLIT PEA AND VEGETABLE SOUP

SERVES 4

1 tablespoon peanut or vegetable oil

1 onion, chopped

2 garlic cloves, chopped

1½ teaspoons chopped fresh ginger

1½ tablespoons Madras curry paste

100 g (3½ oz) yellow split peas, rinsed and drained

1 large zucchini (courgette), peeled and chopped

1 large carrot, roughly chopped

170 g (6 oz) button mushrooms, roughly chopped

1 celery stalk, roughly chopped

1 litre (35 fl oz/4 cups) vegetable stock

125 ml (4 fl oz/½ cup) cream

1   **Heat the oil** in a saucepan, add the onion and cook over low heat for 5 minutes, or until soft. Add the garlic, ginger and curry paste and cook over medium heat for 2 minutes. Stir in the split peas until well coated with paste, then add the zucchini, carrot, mushroom and celery and cook for 2 minutes.

2   **Add the stock,** bring to the boil, then reduce the heat and simmer, partly covered, for 1 hour. Remove from the heat and allow to cool slightly.

3   **Transfer the soup** to a blender or food processor and process in batches until smooth. Return to the pan, stir in the cream and gently heat until warmed through. Serve with naan bread, if desired.

SPICY PUMPKIN AND COCONUT SOUP

SERVES 4

1 small red chilli, seeded and chopped

1 lemongrass stem, white part only, sliced

1 teaspoon ground coriander

1 tablespoon chopped fresh ginger

500 ml (17 fl oz/2 cups) vegetable stock

2 tablespoons oil

1 onion, finely chopped

800 g (1 lb 12 oz) pumpkin (squash) flesh, cubed (see Note)

375 ml (13 oz/1½ cups) coconut milk

3 tablespoons chopped coriander (cilantro) leaves

2 teaspoons shaved palm sugar or soft brown sugar

extra coriander (cilantro) leaves, to garnish

1   Put the chilli, lemon grass, ground coriander, ginger and 2 tablespoons of vegetable stock in a food processor and process until smooth.

2   Heat the oil in a large saucepan over medium heat. Add the onion and cook for 5 minutes. Add the spice paste and cook, stirring, for 1 minute.

3   Add the pumpkin and remaining vegetable stock. Bring to the boil, then reduce the heat and simmer, covered, for 15–20 minutes, or until the pumpkin is tender. Cool slightly, then process in a food processor or blender until smooth. Return to the pan, stir in the coconut milk, coriander and palm sugar and simmer until hot. Garnish with the extra coriander leaves.

Note: You will need to buy 1.5 kg (3 lb 5 oz) pumpkin with the skin on to yield 800 g (1 lb 12 oz) flesh.

VEGETABLE AND LENTIL SOUP WITH SPICED YOGHURT

SERVES 6

2 tablespoons olive oil

1 leek, white part only, chopped

2 garlic cloves, crushed

2 teaspoons curry powder

1 teaspoon ground cumin

1 teaspoon garam masala

1 litre (35 fl oz/4 cups) vegetable stock

1 bay leaf

185 g (6½ oz/1 cup) brown lentils

450 g (1 lb) butternut pumpkin (squash), peeled and cut into 1 cm (½ inch) cubes

2 zucchini (courgettes), cut in half lengthways and sliced

400 g (14 oz) tinned chopped tomatoes

200 g (7 oz) broccoli, cut into small florets

1 small carrot, diced

80 g (2¾ oz/½ cup) peas

1 tablespoon chopped mint

SPICED YOGHURT

250 g (9 oz/1 cup) plain yoghurt

1 tablespoon chopped coriander (cilantro) leaves

1 garlic clove, crushed

3 dashes Tabasco sauce

1 **Heat the oil** in a saucepan over medium heat. Add the leek and garlic and cook for 4 minutes. Add the curry powder, cumin and garam masala and cook for 1 minute. Add the stock, bay leaf, lentils and pumpkin. Bring to the boil, then reduce the heat and simmer for 10–15 minutes, or until the lentils are tender. Season. Add the zucchini, tomatoes, broccoli, carrot and 500 ml (17 fl oz/2 cups) of water and simmer for 10 minutes, or until the vegetables are tender. Add the peas and simmer for 2–3 minutes.

2 **To make** the spiced yoghurt, put the yoghurt, coriander, garlic and Tabasco in a bowl and stir until combined. Serve with the soup and garnish with the mint.

JERUSALEM ARTICHOKE AND ROAST GARLIC SOUP

SERVES 4

1 garlic head

40 g (1½ oz) butter

1 tablespoon olive oil

1 onion, chopped

1 leek, white part only, chopped

1 celery stalk, chopped

700 g (1 lb 9 oz) Jerusalem artichokes, peeled and chopped

1 small potato, chopped

1.5 litres (52 fl oz/6 cups) vegetable or chicken stock

olive oil, to serve

finely chopped chives, to garnish

1 **Preheat the oven** to 200°C (400°F/Gas 6). Slice the base from the head of garlic, wrap it in foil and roast for 30 minutes, or until soft. When cool enough to handle, remove from the foil and slip the cloves from the skin. Set aside.

2 **Heat the butter** and oil in a large heavy-based saucepan over medium heat. Add the onion, leek and celery and a large pinch of salt and cook for 10 minutes, or until soft. Add the Jerusalem artichokes, potato and garlic and cook for a further 10 minutes. Pour in the stock and bring the mixture to the boil. Reduce the heat and simmer for 30 minutes, or until the vegetables are soft.

3 **Purée** the mixture in a blender until smooth, and season well. Serve with a drizzle of olive oil and garnish with chives.

SWEET POTATO AND PEAR SOUP

SERVES 4

25 g (1 oz) butter

1 small white onion, finely chopped

750 g (1 lb 10 oz) orange sweet potato, peeled and cut into 2 cm (¾ inch) cubes

2 firm pears (500 g/1 lb 2 oz), peeled, cored and cut into 2 cm (¾ inch) cubes

750 ml (26 fl oz/3 cups) vegetable or chicken stock

250 ml (9 fl oz/1 cup) cream

mint leaves, to garnish

1 Melt the butter in a saucepan over medium heat. Add the onion and cook for 2–3 minutes, or until softened. Add the sweet potato and pear, and cook, stirring, for 1–2 minutes. Add the stock, bring to the boil and cook for 20 minutes, or until the sweet potato and pear are soft.

2 Cool slightly, then place the mixture in a blender or food processor and blend in batches until smooth. Return to the pan, stir in the cream and gently reheat without boiling. Season and garnish with the mint.

CREAM OF FENNEL AND LEEK SOUP

SERVES 6

30 g (1 oz) butter

2 large fennel bulbs, thinly sliced

2 leeks, thinly sliced

1 litre (35 fl oz/4 cups) hot vegetable or
chicken stock

2 rosemary sprigs

⅛ teaspoon ground nutmeg

80 g (2¾ oz/⅓ cup) sour cream

25 g (1 oz/¼ cup) finely grated
parmesan cheese

1 tablespoon oil

1 leek, extra, cut in half lengthways,
and cut into 4 cm (1½ inch) lengths

grated parmesan cheese, extra,
to garnish

sour cream, extra, to garnish

1 **Heat the butter** in a large heavy-based saucepan and add the sliced fennel and leek. Cook, covered, over medium heat for 2–3 minutes, stirring occasionally.

2 **Put the hot stock,** rosemary sprigs and nutmeg in a saucepan and bring to the boil. Simmer over low heat for about 15 minutes, then remove the rosemary sprigs and add the fennel and leek mixture to the pan.

3 **Transfer the soup** to a blender or food processor and blend in batches until smooth. Return to the pan and stir in the sour cream and parmesan. Reheat over medium heat until hot. Season to taste and keep warm.

4 **Heat the oil** in a frying pan and cook the extra leek for 2–3 minutes, or until soft but not browned.

5 **Top** with the fried leek and garnish with the extra parmesan and sour cream. Serve immediately.

POTATO AND SWEET CORN CHOWDER

SERVES 4

6 sweet corn cobs

2 tablespoons vegetable oil

1 onion, finely diced

3 garlic cloves, crushed

1 celery stalk, diced

1 carrot, peeled and diced

2 large potatoes, peeled and diced

1 litre (35 fl oz/4 cups) vegetable or chicken stock

2 tablespoons finely chopped flat-leaf (Italian) parsley

1 Bring a large saucepan of salted water to the boil. Cook the sweet corn for 5 minutes. Reserve 250 ml (9 fl oz/1 cup) of the cooking water. Cut the corn kernels from the cob, place half in a blender with the reserved cooking water, and blend until smooth.

2 Heat the oil in a large saucepan. Add the onion, garlic, celery and a large pinch of salt and cook for 5 minutes. Add the carrot and potatoes, cook for a further 5 minutes, then add the stock, corn kernels and blended corn mixture. Reduce the heat and simmer for 20 minutes, or until the vegetables are tender. Season well and stir in the chopped parsley before serving.

FRESH MUSHROOM, SHALLOT AND SOUR CREAM SOUP

SERVES 4

40 g (1½ oz) butter

100 g (3½ oz) French shallots, roughly chopped

3 garlic cloves, crushed

30 g (1 oz) flat-leaf (Italian) parsley

315 ml (10¾ fl oz/1¼ cups) vegetable or chicken stock

315 ml (10¾ fl oz/1¼ cups) milk

600 g (1 lb 5 oz) button mushrooms, chopped, plus extra to garnish (optional)

¼ teaspoon ground nutmeg

¼ teaspoon cayenne pepper, plus extra to garnish

150 g (5½ oz) light sour cream

1 **Melt the butter** in a large heavy-based saucepan and add the shallots, garlic and parsley. Cook over medium heat for 2–3 minutes.

2 **Put the stock** and milk in a separate saucepan and bring to the boil.

3 **Add the mushrooms** to the shallot mixture. Season, then stir in the nutmeg and cayenne pepper. Cook, stirring, for 1 minute. Add the stock and milk, bring to the boil, then reduce the heat and simmer for 5 minutes. Transfer the soup to a blender or food processor and blend until smooth. Return to the pan.

4 **Stir in the sour cream** and reheat gently. Season to taste and serve sprinkled with cayenne pepper. Garnish with the extra mushrooms, lightly fried in butter, if desired.

PUMPKIN AND RED LENTIL SOUP

SERVES 4

1 tablespoon olive oil

1 long red chilli, seeded and chopped

1 onion, finely chopped

500 g (1 lb 2 oz) butternut pumpkin (squash), chopped

350 g (12 oz) orange sweet potato, chopped

1.5 litres (52 fl oz/6 cups) vegetable stock

125 g (4½ oz/½ cup) red lentils

1 tablespoon tahini

red chilli, extra, to garnish

1 Heat the oil in a saucepan over medium heat. Add the chilli and onion and cook for 2–3 minutes, or until the onion is soft. Reduce the heat to low, add the pumpkin and sweet potato and cook, covered, for 8 minutes, stirring occasionally.

2 Increase the heat to high, add the stock and bring to the boil. Reduce the heat to low, and simmer, covered, for 10 minutes. Add the red lentils and cook, covered, for 7 minutes, or until tender.

3 Process the soup in batches in a blender or food processor. Add the tahini and blend until smooth. Return to the saucepan and gently heat until warmed through. Garnish with chilli.

CURRIED LENTIL, CARROT AND CASHEW SOUP

SERVES 6

1.5 litres (52 fl oz/6 cups) vegetable or chicken stock

750 g (1 lb 10 oz) carrots, grated

185 g (6½ oz/¾ cup) red lentils, rinsed and drained

1 tablespoon olive oil

1 large onion, chopped

80 g (2¾ oz/½ cup) unsalted cashew nuts

1 tablespoon Madras curry paste

25 g (1 oz) chopped coriander (cilantro) leaves and stems

125 g (4½ oz/½ cup) Greek-style yoghurt

coriander (cilantro) leaves, to garnish

1 Bring the stock to the boil in a large saucepan. Add the carrots and lentils, bring the mixture back to the boil. Simmer over low heat for about 8 minutes, or until the carrot and lentils are soft.

2 Meanwhile, heat the oil in a large frying pan. Add the onion and cashews and cook over medium heat for 2–3 minutes, or until the onion is soft and browned. Add the curry paste and coriander and cook for a further 1 minute, or until fragrant. Stir the paste into the carrot and lentil mixture.

3 Transfer to a food processor or blender and process in batches until smooth. Return the mixture to the pan and reheat over medium heat until hot. Season to taste and serve with a dollop of yoghurt and a sprinkling of coriander.

Note: Garnish the soup with a pinch of chilli flakes to give it an extra kick.

THAI SPICY SOUR SOUP

750 ml (26 fl oz/3 cups) vegetable stock

2 tablespoons tom yum paste
(see Note)

2 cm x 2 cm (¾ inch x ¾ inch) piece
galangal, peeled and cut into
thin slices

1 lemongrass stem, lightly crushed and
cut into 4 lengths

3 kaffir lime leaves

1 small red chilli, finely sliced on the
diagonal (optional)

200 g (7 oz) button mushrooms, halved

200 g (7 oz) silken firm tofu, cut into
1.5 cm (⅝ inch) cubes

200 g (7 oz) baby bok choy (pak choy),
roughly shredded

2 tablespoons lime juice

1 small handful coriander
(cilantro) leaves

1 Place the stock, tom yum paste, galangal, lemon grass, kaffir lime leaves, chilli and 750 ml (26 fl oz/3 cups) of water in a saucepan. Cover and bring to the boil, then reduce the heat and simmer for 5 minutes.

2 Add the mushrooms and tofu and simmer for 5 minutes, or until the mushrooms are tender. Add the bok choy and simmer for a further minute, or until wilted. Remove the pan from the heat and stir in the lime juice and coriander leaves before serving.

Note: For vegetarian cooking, buy a brand of tom yum paste that does not contain shrimp paste or fish sauce.

LAKSA

SERVES 4

200 g (7 oz) dried rice vermicelli

2 tablespoons peanut oil

2–3 tablespoons laksa paste

1 litre (35 fl oz/4 cups) vegetable stock

750 ml (26 fl oz/3 cups) coconut milk

250 g (9 oz) snow peas (mangetout),
   halved diagonally

5 spring onions (scallions), cut into
   3 cm (1¼ inch) lengths

2 tablespoons lime juice

125 g (4½ oz) bean sprouts, trimmed

200 g (7 oz) fried tofu puffs, halved

3 tablespoons roughly chopped
   Vietnamese mint

20 g (¾ oz) coriander (cilantro) leaves

1 **Put the vermicelli** in a large bowl, cover with boiling water and soak for 5 minutes.

2 **Heat the oil** in a large saucepan, add the laksa paste and cook, stirring, over medium heat for 1 minute, or until fragrant. Add the stock, coconut milk, snow peas and spring onion and simmer for 5 minutes. Pour in the lime juice and season to taste.

3 **Drain** the vermicelli and add the bean sprouts and fried tofu puffs. Ladle the hot soup over the vermicelli. Serve immediately, sprinkled with the mint and coriander.

CARAMELIZED ONION AND PARSNIP SOUP

SERVES 4

30 g (1 oz) butter

3 large onions, halved and thinly sliced

2 tablespoons soft brown sugar

250 ml (9 fl oz/1 cup) dry white wine

3 large parsnips, peeled, chopped

1.25 litres (44 fl oz/5 cups)
   vegetable stock

3 tablespoons cream

thyme leaves, to garnish

1 Melt the butter in a large saucepan. Add the onion and sugar, and cook over low heat for 10 minutes. Add the wine and parsnip, and simmer, covered, for 20 minutes, or until the onion and parsnip are golden and tender.

2 Pour in the stock, bring to the boil, then reduce the heat and simmer, covered, for 10 minutes. Cool slightly, then place in a blender or food processor and blend in batches until smooth. Season and drizzle with a little cream. Sprinkle the thyme leaves over the top.

LENTIL SOUP

SERVES 4

2 tablespoons olive oil

1 onion, finely chopped

1 leek, finely chopped

4 garlic cloves, finely chopped

1 tablespoon garam masala

1 celery stalk, finely diced

1 carrot, finely diced

230 g (8 oz/1¼ cups) brown lentils

400 g (14 oz) tinned chopped tomatoes

1 tablespoon tomato paste
(concentrated purée)

1.75 litres (61 fl oz/7 cups) chicken or
vegetable stock

2 large sprigs thyme

2 tablespoons chopped parsley, to serve

grated parmesan cheese, to serve

1 **Heat the oil** in a large heavy-based saucepan. Add the onion, leek and garlic. Cook and stir for 2 minutes. Add the garam masala and cook for a further 2 minutes. Stir in the celery and carrot. Cover and cook, stirring two or three times, over low heat for 10 minutes, or until the vegetables are softened.

2 **Add the lentils** and stir to coat in the vegetables. Add the tomatoes, tomato paste, stock and thyme sprigs. Bring to the boil, then lower the heat and simmer for 50 minutes, stirring occasionally, or until the lentils are tender. If evaporating too rapidly, add a little more stock or water to keep the lentils covered with liquid. Remove the thyme sprigs. Season well with salt and black pepper. Serve hot sprinkled with parsley and parmesan.

Note: This soup is very thick, you can thin it with a little stock or water if desired.

GARLIC SOUP

SERVES 4

1 whole bulb garlic (about 20 cloves)

2 large sprigs thyme

1 litres (30 fl oz/4 cups) chicken stock

80 ml (3 fl oz/⅓ cup) cream

salt and white pepper

fresh thyme, to garnish

CHEESE CROUTONS

½ baguette, sliced

50 g (1¾ oz) gruyère cheese, grated

1 **Crush each clove of garlic** with the side of a knife. Discard the skin and place the garlic in a large pan with the thyme, stock and 250 ml (8 fl oz/1 cup) water. Bring to the boil and then reduce the heat and simmer gently for 20 minutes, uncovered.

2 **Strain the soup** through a fine sieve into a clean pan. Add the cream and reheat gently, without allowing to boil. Season to taste.

3 **To make the cheese croutons,** preheat the grill (broiler) and lightly toast the bread on both sides. Sprinkle with the cheese and grill until melted.

4 **To serve,** place a few croutons in each warm bowl and ladle the soup over the top, or serve the croutons on the side.

Note: Best served the same day. The bread cubes may be cooked up to 4 hours in advance and kept in an airtight container until required. The after-effects of the garlic are at a minimum because it has been boiled. In the Mediterranean this soup is considered good for the health.

BARLEY SOUP WITH GOLDEN PARSNIPS

SERVES 6

200 g (6½ oz) pearl barley

1 tablespoon oil

2 onions, chopped

2 cloves garlic, finely chopped

2 carrots, chopped

2 potatoes, chopped

2 celery sticks, chopped

2 bay leaves, torn in half

2 litres chicken stock

125 ml (4 fl oz/ ½ cup) milk

40 g (1¼ oz) butter

3 parsnips, cubed

1 teaspoon soft brown sugar

chopped fresh parsley, to serve

1 Soak the barley in water overnight. Drain. Place in a saucepan with 2 litres water. Bring to the boil, then reduce the heat and simmer, partially covered, for 1¼ hours, or until tender. Drain the barley.

2 Heat the oil in a large saucepan, add the onion, garlic, carrot, potato and celery, and cook for 3 minutes. Stir well and cook, covered, for 15 minutes over low heat, stirring occasionally.

3 Add the barley, bay leaves, stock, milk, 2 teaspoons of salt and 1 teaspoon of freshly ground black pepper. Bring to the boil, then reduce the heat and simmer the soup, partially covered, for 35 minutes. If the soup is too thick, add about 1 cup (250 ml/8 fl oz) cold water, a little at a time, until the soup reaches your preferred consistency.

4 While the soup is simmering, melt the butter in a frying pan, add the parsnip and toss in the butter. Sprinkle with the sugar and cook until golden brown and tender.

5 Serve the parsnip on top of the soup and sprinkle with the parsley.

Note: The soup will keep in the refrigerator, covered, for up to 4 days, or in an airtight container in the freezer for up to 1 month.

GREAT TASTES SOUPS

TOMATO SOUP

SERVES 4

20 g (¾ oz) unsalted butter

1 celery stalk, finely chopped

1 onion, finely chopped

1 carrot, finely chopped

1 garlic clove, crushed

700 g (1 lb 9 oz/2¾ cups)
tomato-based pasta sauce

750 ml (26 fl oz/3 cups) salt-reduced
chicken or vegetable stock

1 teaspoon sugar

1 parsley sprig

1 bay leaf

250 ml (9 fl oz/1 cup) milk

2 teaspoons chopped parsley

toast, to serve

1 **Melt the butter** in a saucepan and sauté the celery, onion and carrot for 3–4 minutes. Add the garlic and cook for 30 seconds. Add the pasta sauce, chicken or vegetable stock, sugar, parsley sprig and bay leaf. Bring to the boil, then simmer for 10 minutes. Remove the parsley and bay leaf.

2 **Purée the soup** in a blender, then return it to the pan. Stir through the milk and heat until hot.

3 **Garnish with the parsley** and serve with toast.

INDEX

GREAT TASTES SOUPS